And Their Works
Do Follow Them

Blessed are the dead which die in the Lord:
they rest from their labours
and their works do follow them.

The inscription on Frances Mary Buss's tombstone
in Theydon Bois churchyard.

AND THEIR WORKS DO FOLLOW THEM

*The Story of
North London Collegiate School*

Nigel Watson

Foreword

'Why are women so little thought of? I want girls educated to match their brothers!'

When Frances Mary Buss expressed her frustration at the poor state of women's education, girls were expected to acquire only those accomplishments that would make them good companions for men and suitable ornaments for the home. Given the difficulties she had to overcome because of the prejudices of the age she lived in, and given there was nothing remarkable in her own education, it is extraordinary that she achieved, with such spectacular success, what is now recognised as *the* major step forward in the schooling and thence the condition of women.

Miss Buss's genius lay in making her ideas work; in 1850 she had no model to copy, no precedent of any kind. She had to think of how to implement women's education: how to encourage parental support, what kind of curriculum to offer and how to supervise and manage her School. It seems to me her major achievements were twofold: first, she created something from nothing and secondly, in the process of doing so, she instituted many of the elements that we regard as essential in the running of a good school today. She insisted on treating her teachers as professionals and involving them in discussions of policy; she was clear that teaching methods must take account of the response of the individual pupil; rote learning and a slavish adherence to text books were discouraged. And she was prepared to change, with a commitment to continuous improvement that foreshadowed the approaches of our public services today.

Remarkable though these features of her work were, the most enduring aspect of her legacy seems to me to be her firm commitment to the idea that the talents of all her students should be recognised, and that even those in difficulties should be given encouragement to exceed previous expectations. It is a rare testimony to the power of her vision that this single-minded determination to help each pupil to realise her potential has remained a guiding principle for all subsequent Head Mistresses. It also explains not only the remarkable academic record of the School, but also the high degree of affection in which the School is held by generations of Old North Londoners.

The admiration for Miss Buss's achievements I felt reading all that had been written about her became more meaningful for me on a Sunday afternoon late in February of this year when I decided to visit her grave. As I walked alone around the churchyard in Theydon Bois, among the lichen-covered gravestones that slant with age, searching for the grave of the woman who lay buried there, I reflected on whether she would recognise North London Collegiate School today.

And I felt quite sure that, because of the efforts and commitment to her ideals of generations of Head Mistresses and their staff, that she would see sustained in today's school the principles she fought so hard for: the achievement of academic excellence, with no ambition or career closed to young women; a strong awareness of the need for the cultural side of life to bring balance and refreshment. How impressed she would be by the extraordinary range of facilities now offered to our pupils, compared with the cramped buildings she coped with. She would have been delighted, I hope, by the variety of extra-curricular opportunities there are for our students today: music, sport, drama, dance, debating, more than twenty clubs and societies, and residential educational visits at home and abroad for the pupils each holiday. And I am sure she would have applauded the current Bursary Appeal, for we are still determined to keep the social mix she wished for her School and to provide an education for able girls irrespective of their parents' ability to pay our fees.

This remarkable woman could have had no real idea whether her pioneering vision would be a success, when she died worn out with her efforts in 1894. If she were with us today, she could take comfort in the knowledge that not only does North London Collegiate School flourish (and has been named Independent School of the Year by the national press) but that other schools and institutions across the country have been inspired by her vision, and by her discipline and determination in translating this vision into reality.

I stood for a while beside the pink mottled granite tombstone behind the church in Theydon Bois. And as I left the darkening cemetery on that February afternoon the simple inscription on her grave struck me as entirely appropriate: 'Blessed are the dead which die in the Lord: they rest from their labours and their works do follow them.'

The final words of this epitaph have been chosen as a title for this book, because they reflect the influence of past Head Mistresses, teachers and pupils; they also echo the way Old North Londoners have demonstrated Miss Buss's pioneering spirit in their lives and in their contribution to society.

Nigel Watson had no previous connection with NLCS when he undertook this commission. His scholarly work is the result of many hours immersed in the School archive combined with interviews of Head Mistresses past and present. He has combined successfully a detailed historical account with a perceptive appreciation of the characters that have shaped the School over 150 years. He was quick to identify the unique spirit and energy of NLCS and his text admirably communicates the way in which subsequent Head Mistresses have interpreted Miss Buss's vision for the education of women.

We are also very grateful to Karen Morgan, our archivist, and the team of librarians who helped Nigel with his research. We are also indebted to Ennis Brandenburger, herself an ONL and ex-governor, for all her help and attention to detail in reading the proofs.

Bernice McCabe
Head Mistress
April 2000

Acknowledgements

The task of writing the history of the North London Collegiate School was a challenge which gave me a great deal of pleasure. It is a remarkable school, located in a remarkable environment, which has been led by some remarkable women. I only hope that this book does the School justice.

The book could not have been completed without the willing help and advice of a number of people. Firstly, I would like to say thank you to those who kindly allowed me to interview them for the history, including Joan Lundie, Norma Rinsler, Ann Thomas, Robyn Townley and especially three past and present Head Mistresses, Madeline McLauchlan, Joan Clanchy and Bernice McCabe. At the School I was well looked after by Barbara Pomeroy, Judy Dudley and the staff of the School library. I would like to say a particular thank you to Ennis Brandenburger whose most perceptive comments on the draft have made this a better book than it began. I would also like to thank Hamish MacGibbon of James & James for asking me to take on such a fascinating project.

After completing the book I was kindly invited to attend the Sesquicentenary Founder's Day Service. The Head Mistress's address fittingly paid tribute to Frances Mary Buss after which the School and those guests at the service took part in the daffodil procession, remembering not only her great achievements but also those of her successors. Having come to know so much about Miss Buss, her successors and the School, I found it a moving experience which reaffirmed for me the strength of the human dimension which has made the North London Collegiate School such a unique institution.

Nigel Watson
Spring 2000

Contents

Prize Day, 1857, held in the garden (note the see-saw).

1

'A Sound and Liberal Education'
1850–80

Time was when very little reading, plain work, pudding making and pickling constituted the amount of education of a girl of the middle classes.

Prize Day Report, Christmas 1850.

When North London Collegiate School welcomed its first pupils on 4 April 1850, it began a process of fundamental change in girls' education. The fact that the School existed at all owed everything to the deplorable state of girls' education in the middle of the nineteenth century and to the single-minded determination of Frances Mary Buss to change it. Under this remarkable woman, the School established a reputation based on inspired leadership, talented staff and an expectation of the highest standards from its pupils which remain characteristics of the School today. This reputation did not come easily. The effort poured into her work by Miss Buss to overcome the enormous prejudice which existed against girls' education in Victorian England cost her both her wealth and her health. But together with her friend and ally in the cause, Dorothea Beale, Miss Buss is recognised today as the pioneer of girls' secondary education. North London Collegiate School is not only a monument to her work, it is also a living testament to the achievement of her successors in keeping this remarkable School at the forefront of girls' education.

Among the reasons which propelled Frances Mary Buss into teaching, two are particularly striking. Firstly, since her father's earnings as an artist, engraver and illustrator were unpredictable, she and the other members of her close-knit family had to employ their talents in securing a more regular income for the household. Secondly, teaching was one of the few career opportunities open to her as a middle-class Victorian woman. Throughout her life, Miss Buss, in striving for her ideals, always recognised the commercial realities, even if she sometimes chose to ignore them.

R. W. Buss, Frances Mary's father, photographed by himself in the 1850s.

Born in London on 16 August 1827, she was the eldest child and only surviving daughter of Robert William Buss and his wife, Frances. Robert, an amiable, modest and gentle man, was a talented and imaginative artist. Invited to produce etchings for the *Pickwick Papers* in 1836, his lack of experience as an engraver let him down. But he learnt from this lesson and in the following year went on to produce much praised illustrations for Captain Marryat's *Peter Simple*, which led to a number of further commissions. His engravings were popular and sold well and he also lectured on art and art history. His daughter inherited his love of art, history and reading, as well as his penchant for amateur theatricals. Robert's wife, Frances, was the perfect counterfoil to her husband. A loving and warm-hearted person, she was also strong, resourceful and practical, a description which could be applied equally to Frances Mary.

Frances Mary's childhood in her Mornington Crescent home was a happy one and in her professional career she placed great emphasis on the importance of home life for her pupils. She saw no reason why any girl should be taken from the formative influences of her home at an early age to be despatched to some far-flung and often uncongenial boarding school.

Her own education was taken locally. From a small dame school run by Miss Cook, she went on to attend the school run by Mrs Wyand in Mornington Place, Hampstead Road. Mrs Wyand was a small but commanding figure, whose dignity and authority Frances Mary sought to

Dickens' Dream, *by R. W. Buss.*

recapture through her own appearance. The importance of establishing a sense of presence was brought home to her at an early age since she began teaching in the school at the age of 14. By the time she was 16 she was sometimes left in sole charge of a class for a week at a time.

At the age of 18 she left Mrs Wyand's establishment, where she had excelled in French, to join her mother who was opening a preparatory school for young children at 14 Clarence Road in Kentish Town. Unlike most of those running similar schools, Mrs Buss prepared for her new venture by attending a course of instruction at the Home and Colonial Society in Gray's Inn Road, a commitment which impressed itself on her daughter. Working alongside her mother, Frances Mary taught a small number of young ladies every morning. The course she offered them included English, French, geography, history, art, science, writing, arithmetic and fancy needlework. Music, dancing, Latin, German and Italian were available as extras. The prospectus shrewdly stated that 'The Course of Education proposed will combine the usual Accomplishments with the essential points of a liberal education.' Several of the subjects being offered by Mrs and Miss Buss were found only rarely in the education offered to middle-class girls; more usually the emphasis was on needlework, dancing and music. So here was contained not only the germ of the secondary education for which the North London Collegiate School later became renowned, Miss Buss was also ensuring that by stressing the continuance of the 'usual Accomplishments' and underplaying the 'liberal education' by providing only its 'essential points' she would not deter those conservatively minded middle-class fathers who held the purse strings from sending their daughters to the Clarence Road school.

The general standard of education for middle-class girls in the 1840s was abysmal. Unlike working-class girls, whose education was supposed to train them for work in domestic service or as the wives of working-class men, girls of the upper and middle classes were expected to acquire only those accomplishments which would fit them for their wifely roles as ornaments within the home: 'Gentle trills on the piano, a little conversational French, a charming song or two, sketches of picturesque ruins and some delicate tapestry work.' When Miss Buss began teaching at Clarence Road, views on the role of married women were beginning to change. Rather than being regarded as inferior dependants, they were seen within marriage more as equals and friends. But this was still a minority opinion in a male-dominated world which regarded women as morally superior but intellectually inferior to men. The logic of this argument, which had widespread support among many women as well as most men, was that there was little point in teaching girls subjects like French or German or Italian which they would be unable to use. So there was very little attempt to impart genuine learning. The preferred alternative was to spoon-feed pupils vast quantities of trivial information through useless catechisms and

Frances Mary Buss aged 33.

North London Collegiate School at 46 Camden Street, 1850. In 1864 no 46 was renumbered to become nos 12 and 14.

11

Traditional female accomplishments in the mid-nineteenth century: reading, embroidery and playing the piano.

F. D. Maurice: pioneer of education for girls.

epitomes for learning by rote. Frederick Denison Maurice, Professor of English Literature and Modern History at King's College, London, who was to play a key role in developing women's education, wrote in 1826 that 'The imagination is a terrible object of the dread, the hatred and hostility of the mistresses of establishments and the governesses of young ladies.' Given this low attachment to feminine middle-class education by both men and women, it was scarcely surprising that the quality of many of those schools which did exist was poor. It was said that the instruction in accomplishments in which many of these schools were supposed to specialise often left their pupils unable to sing, dance, draw or paint with any competence.

This practice began to change mainly because of a concern for those women who remained unmarried in spite of their education. Previously such middle-class spinsters had been supported financially by their families for whom the idea that their single daughters should earn their own living was inconceivable. But such support, even though it publicly indicated a certain level of wealth, was expensive. As such numbers of women increased during the first half of the nineteenth century, so the idea that they should pay their own way in the world became more

12

acceptable. The problem which now arose was that there had never been many opportunities for such women and those which did exist were poorly paid and badly regarded.

Many spinsters whose families could no longer afford to support them became governesses. In 1843 the Governesses' Benevolent Institution had been formed in Harley Street with the intention of raising their status in order to improve their pitiful salaries. It was quickly realised that one way of achieving this would be to remedy their lack of education. Professor Maurice arranged for himself and a group of academic colleagues to deliver lectures for these young women in a house adjacent to the Institution and these were formalised in 1848 with the establishment of Queen's College. Although primarily intended for governesses, the courses, which encompassed a curriculum so broad it was regarded as radical, were open to all women over the age of 12. The College was an enormous success with 200 applicants during its first term.

The Honorary Secretary of the Governesses' Benevolent Institution was David Laing, the vicar of Holy Trinity, Haverstock Hill. A wealthy, cultured and liberal man, who devoted his personal fortune to the foundation and development of his parish, he knew Frances Mary Buss from visiting the school in Clarence Road and from her attendance at his church. He became the greatest influence on Miss Buss during her early life and he encouraged her to attend the new lectures being given at Queen's College. Miss Buss needed little persuasion. She was aware of her own educational deficiencies and of the benefit which her mother had drawn from the training course she had attended at the Home and Colonial Society. Miss Buss took evening classes at the College, gaining certificates in French, German and geography during 1849 and 1850. Among her fellow pupils were Dorothea Beale, whom she did not meet until much later, and Elizabeth Day, who became the first head mistress of Manchester High School. Queen's College and Bedford College, established at the same time for the same purpose, 'provided a cadre of women who were capable of running schools for girls that could provide an education comparable with the public schools at which their brothers were taught.'

At the age of 22, Frances Mary Buss was already armed with eight years' teaching experience. With the certificates gained from Queen's College, she now felt more confident about her own intellectual capacity. The atmosphere at the College had also increased her own enthusiasm for pushing further forward her developing ideas for the education of girls. In the spring of 1850, this ambitious young woman issued a prospectus for the North London Collegiate School for Ladies.

The imposing name was taken from a neighbouring school which had recently opened for boys. The School's patrons consisted of the vicar and clergy of St Pancras, including David Laing. The School had the benefit of

Dr David Laing: an important influence on Frances Mary Buss, he encouraged her to enter education.

Frances Mary Buss's certificate for German, gained at Queen's College in 1848.

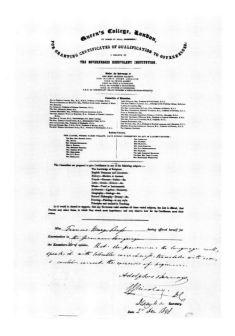

13

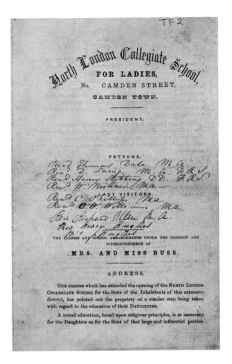

The 1850 prospectus.

The first North Londoners outside the Camden Street school, 1850.

the early and sustained aristocratic interest of the Countess of Hardwicke, a known sympathiser in the cause of girls' education. These measures, in creating at once a respectable impression of the School attractive to her middle-class catchment area, exemplified Miss Buss's shrewd political instincts. She was keenly aware that her efforts could never succeed unless she retained the support of the conservative middle-class men who were either fathers or officials or figures of influence. In this instance her target was the professional middle classes of Camden, 'Professional Gentlemen of limited means, Clerks in public and private Offices, and Persons engaged in trade and other pursuits.' As she pointed out in her Prize Day Report in 1852, 'Of all the vast suburbs of our vast metropolis, this district . . . is perhaps more thickly inhabited by Professional man than any other.' To suit their pockets, fees were set at two guineas a quarter.

While accomplishments still formed part of the education offered by the School, the emphasis was now more firmly on 'the essential branches of a sound and liberal education upon religious principles.' The curriculum was based largely on that adopted at Mrs Buss's Clarence Road school although Latin was now part of the core curriculum rather than an optional extra. The aim of the new School was ostensibly modest: to educate future mothers so that they might 'diffuse amongst their children the truths and duties of religion' and 'impart to them a portion of that mass of information placed by modern education within the reach of all.' But the school motto, 'We work in hope', implicitly indicated higher ambitions.

The Clarence Road school had moved in 1849 to larger premises in Holmes Terrace where Mr Buss and his sons, Alfred and Septimus, had been called upon to assist Mrs Buss with teaching. In a short time, however, Mrs Buss gave up her preparatory school. The North London Collegiate School began life on 4 April 1850 in the Buss family home in 46 Camden Street, with thirty-eight pupils. The family occupied the basement and attics while the parlour acted as Miss Buss's room during school hours between ten in the morning and three in the afternoon.

Sara Burstall, a later pupil of the School, recorded that 'This early school was her laboratory, where she worked out experimentally the plans to be developed on a large scale after 1871 and to be the models for the day school system.' This was true; Miss Buss foresaw the fashionable 1990s theory of 'continuous improvement' nearly 150 years earlier, writing in 1850 that 'Wherever improvement can be introduced, it will be immediately adopted.' Nevertheless, despite continuous evolution, many of the fundamental characteristics of the School at its beginning have lasted to this day.

From the start the School was intended to cater for girls from every level of the broad Victorian middle class. This was dictated partly by the School's location, partly by the need to fill the School, but also because of Miss Buss's deeply held belief that as many middle-class girls as possible should be able to benefit from a sound education. So the emphasis was always upon moderate fees to enable fathers to send all their daughters to the School. For middle-class families with both sons and daughters where the priority was nearly always their sons' education, this was an important consideration. The level of fees was certainly one reason why the School had grown by Christmas 1851 to 115 pupils drawn from a wide variety of backgrounds: forty-four fathers were gentlemen, twenty-six were in trade, fourteen were clerks, another fourteen were artists, seven were solicitors, five physicians and surgeons, three clergy and two musicians. Miss Buss insisted that girls from every background were treated exactly the same and this lack of social distinction, albeit among girls from broadly the same social class, became a defining feature of the North London Collegiate School.

The School inculcated an ethos of religious as well as social tolerance. Miss Buss welcomed girls from the local Jewish community and from Roman Catholic families. When one Jewish girl explained to her the significance of High Holy days and her inability to attend school on those days, North London Collegiate became the first school which taught religion according to the Church of England to respect Jewish observances. Although Lucy Henry, who entered the School in 1865, and her sister were for a time the only Jewish children in the School, Miss Buss nevertheless ensured that daily attendance was called for after prayers rather than before as had previously been the case. Roman Catholics were also permitted to absent themselves from morning prayers. (Miss Buss was blind to race as well: the daughter of a black Jamaican merchant entered the School in the 1870s.)

Miss Buss was alert to the social sensibilities of the parents of her pupils. The objects of the School set out in the summer of 1850 could as yet see pupils only as 'mothers, sisters or governesses' whose education should 'fit them for the important position in society they will be called upon to occupy'; while the system for teaching the youngest pupils (who were admitted in the School's early years from the time they could walk) was drawn from the elementary schools 'but so modified as to be adapted to the rank in life of the young ladies who are pupils.' Miss Buss cleverly used Victorian class distinctions to win over potential parents with the argument that since working-class girls were being educated so well in the National Schools, it was imperative for middle-class girls to become better educated 'or they would be found more ignorant than their servants'. An added attraction for fathers who may have dreaded the future cost of maintaining any unmarried daughters was that the School offered an education deliberately designed to be suitable for intending governesses who wished to move on to Queen's College.

The limited horizons of the mid-Victorian woman were reflected in Miss Buss's comment at Prize Day in 1853 that 'This course of study is one

Alfred J. Buss, Frances Mary's brother, and Clerk to the Governors for many years.

Septimus Buss, another brother, who taught scripture and drawing at the School.

15

which if terminated at 14 or 16 years of age will be found sufficient to render the pupil fit for any society.' Sadly, many girls in the School's early years left prematurely but this only made Miss Buss more determined to provide them as far as possible with 'a thorough education'. Although North London Collegiate gained a reputation in some quarters in later years for being the school where girls were prepared for earning their living, that was only ever one part of Miss Buss's view of education. She was equally determined that an education at the School should enable a girl both to lead a life worth living and to enrich the world around her. This has remained a central tradition of the School to this day.

One acceptable occupation for married Victorian women was an involvement in philanthropic works. This interest was cultivated at North London Collegiate School because it was worth doing for its own sake and an ethic of social service became one of the School's distinguishing attributes. At Christmas 1850 parents were told that the girls, 'combining the useful with the ornamental', would be making clothes for local charities, an activity formalised with the creation of the Dorcas Society in 1858, when a Juvenile Visiting Society was also established for taking 'small comforts' to the poor.

Miss Buss also took into consideration another concern of potential parents. Health, in an age of high mortality, was a major anxiety; later the alleged strain which education imposed on the health of girls would be a main plank of the arguments advanced in the conservative backlash against women's education. Miss Buss took her first steps to pre-empt such criticism before the end of 1850, ensuring that pupils had somewhere to get themselves dry if they were caught in a downpour before they got to school, and that they were properly fed during the day.

But while the School did as much as possible to attract and retain the support of local middle-class parents by taking into account their income, their social sensibilities and their anxieties, these were by no means its only defining characteristics. It also set out to offer their daughters an education quite different from anything available anywhere else.

There was, for example, the inclusion of science within the curriculum. Science was not really taken seriously by most girls' schools until well into the twentieth century. Robert Buss made a memorable science teacher as Annie Martinelli, an early pupil, later remembered: 'His talents were simply wonderful. His delightful lectures in Botany, Zoology, Geology and Astronomy were illustrated with profuse diagrams. His Chemistry series was marvellous, especially for smells and explosions.' He was the first of a series of outstanding science teachers at the School where learning by rote was replaced from the beginning by encouraging pupils to learn by thinking for themselves.

Conscious of her own experience as a teacher, as well as the example of her mother, Frances Mary Buss also insisted that all the teaching staff

Maria Buss, an early pupil and teacher at North London, who married her cousin Septimus.

16

'The Morning Drive',
46 Camden Street, c. 1850.

at the School should be trained at the Home and Colonial Society. Initially this was the only way she could obtain any qualified staff. Such a route was followed by two of the School's first pupils, Maria Buss and Eleanor Begbie. In Maria's case, she completed her school education at the age of 16 in 1852 before training at the Home and Colonial and joining the teaching staff at the School. This set a pattern for the future with many pupils taking advantage of the increasing opportunities in higher education which became available during the second half of the century to obtain further academic and teaching qualifications before returning to serve at North London Collegiate.

For all these reasons and more, the School appealed to the professional middle class of Camden and the number of pupils soon climbed to around 200, as many as the Camden Street building could accommodate. The broad social intake was maintained and parental occupations in 1865 ranged from doctors and dentists to Meerschaum pipe importers and a cricket warehouseman by the name of Lillywhite! Despite the moderate fees (which had risen modestly to three guineas a quarter by 1865), there were always those unable to afford the total cost. Six scholarships were established in memory of David Laing after his death in 1860 while others were left to the discretion of 'the Mistress'.

Many girls were now travelling 'long distances' and for some of them limited boarding accommodation was made available. The sole boarding house was taken over by Miss Buss in 1866 and moved to a property closer to the School, while a second one was opened shortly afterwards under the care of the Misses Smith at 15 Camden Road. Miss Buss, however, disliked boarding schools which gave 'a sort of hardness . . . They destroy home-feelings . . . my feelings are most in favour of day schools and good homes.' Because of this, and so that a domestic atmosphere could be maintained in the boarding houses, numbers were kept small. Miss Buss also insisted on the clear separation between the boarding houses and the School, with all boarders attending the School as day pupils.

On average there were some twenty-five pupils per class with promotion being determined by half-termly marks and examinations. Parents were kept in touch with their daughters' progress through a system of regular monthly progress reports required to be signed and returned to the School. Prizes were awarded twice a year until 1855, the ceremony being held in a large tent in the spacious garden at the rear of the School. In 1862 Prize Day was held for the first time in the St Pancras Vestry Hall. Prizes were given not only to those with the highest marks but also to those who had reached 'a certain fixed standard'.

The school staff was made up of a number of full-time assistant mistresses, still known as 'governesses', and part-time masters, attending when required. As numbers grew, so the Ladies' Principal, as Miss Buss was known, started regular weekly staff meetings as a means of securing 'uniformity of action and exact teaching'. The staff maintained discipline not through the corporal punishment common in boys' schools but through the deduction of marks or, in graver cases, memorised impositions. There were monitors to take charge of new pupils but they had no powers. The plethora of rules characteristic of the School in the later nineteenth century had not yet evolved.

Although the school day in the 1860s had lengthened, beginning at 9.45 a.m. and ending at 4.00 p.m., there were 'no particular games', which were still generally perceived as being too stressful for young women, although the rear gardens were used as playgrounds, and callisthenics or musical gymnastics were practised in the gymnasium. There was a constant emphasis on health. In 1866 Dr Hodgson gave his second series of lectures on health and the human body and in 1868 a physiology course, covering circulation, respiration, nutrition, secretion and excretion, the nervous system and senses, was given to senior girls by Miss Chessar of the Home and Colonial Schools.

Drama was introduced in the form of *tableaux vivants* with the first one being performed in December 1865. These stemmed from the amateur dramatics which had been performed in the Buss household during Frances Mary's childhood. Annie Ridley in her biography of Miss Buss describes one performed in 1869 which reveals Miss Buss's ability to laugh at herself: 'At the close of a series of very artistic pictures, the curtain rose on a concourse of European nations, and Britannia, coming to life, advanced to the front, with an appeal:

> There was an old woman who lived in a shoe,
> She had so many daughters, she didn't know what to do;
> For they all of them possibly couldn't be wed,
> So she gave them a good education instead.'

On the other hand, there was very little musical activity. Miss Buss's hatred at the time of the way instrumental music was then taught in girls' schools, which she condemned as a waste of time and money, left it in the hands of private teachers rather than as a part of the curriculum.

The School remained an oasis in the educational desert: the poverty of the education being given to girls before they came to North London Collegiate meant that new entrants were 'rarely well prepared'. But Miss Buss was disturbed to discover in 1863 that her own school could do better in the way girls were taught and, of course, she found this unacceptable.

This revelation came about through the opening up of external examinations to girls. This itself stemmed from the failure of women to gain admission to the universities. Two attempts to persuade London University to admit women in 1856 and 1862 had both failed. The latter, lost on the casting vote of the chairman of Convocation, had ended the efforts of Elizabeth Garrett, later a Governor of North London Collegiate, to gain a medical degree. One of the arguments used in defence of this decision was that most women were poorly educated and therefore incapable of taking a degree course. There was some merit in this and it prompted Emily Davies, a friend and supporter of Elizabeth Garrett, to press Cambridge University to allow girls to sit the Cambridge University Senior Local Examinations. If these were opened up, they would act as a spur to better education for more women. After long deliberation, the University agreed but gave Emily Davies only three months to find sufficient candidates. The calibre of the candidates was critical since any substantial degree of failure would only reinforce the arguments of opponents to a more enlightened education for women.

Emily Davies turned to her friend, Frances Mary Buss. Miss Buss was hesitant at first but submitted twenty-five candidates from the North London Collegiate School out of a total of ninety-one who sat those first examinations in December 1863. The results finally dispelled the idea that girls would be unable to take the strain of sitting examinations and for the

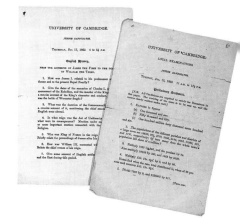

Two Cambridge Local Examination papers.

Emily Davies, who established Girton College, Cambridge, in 1869 and pushed hard for key reforms in the education of young women.

Dorothea Beale, another key figure in the progress of women's education. She was the first Principal of Cheltenham Ladies' College, and the first chairwoman of the Association of Head Mistresses.

first time set an external standard by which all girls' schools might be measured. They were also good enough to persuade the University to permit girls for a further three-year trial period to take the same subjects, work to the same syllabus and sit the same examinations as boys, a radical break with tradition. In 1867 the admission of girls became permanent.

Despite this great achievement, there was one area of performance which caused Frances Mary Buss considerable disappointment. This lay in the arithmetic results. Ten of the North London Collegiate students failed this subject, with fifty-seven out of the ninety-one students from all schools failing. Miss Buss had underestimated both the lack of knowledge of girls on entering the School and the inadequacy of the School's teaching thereafter. She was determined to put things right. In 1866 she proudly reported that 123 of the 126 girls from all schools had passed the arithmetic examination and not one North Londoner had failed. Ten years after that, only two out of North London Collegiate's fifty-three candidates failed the arithmetic examination, 'far less than in any other School, boys or girls'.

For Miss Buss, this lesson convinced her of the value of external examinations. When she was asked by the Schools Inquiry Commission in November 1865 whether the extension of the Cambridge Local Examinations to girls had been beneficial, she replied 'I am quite sure that great good has been done already. An intense stimulus has been given, especially to English and arithmetic. The girls have something to work for, some hope, something to aim for, and the teachers also.' She also stressed that the examinations demonstrated that girls were just as intellectually capable as boys and there was no reason why they should not both enjoy the same education. For her, a separate examination for girls was now meaningless since it had no point of comparison. On the other hand, a concentration on arithmetic arising from the failures of 1863 meant that there was still no place in the curriculum for a complete course in mathematics. Miss Buss told the Commission that she felt maths was simply beyond her girls at this stage.

Miss Buss's involvement with the Schools Inquiry Commission was another triumph both for herself and for the School. Emily Davies had first persuaded the Commission to broaden its remit to inquire into girls' schools and then convinced both Miss Buss and Miss Beale, the latter now in charge of Cheltenham Ladies' College, to open their schools for inspection by the Commission. They were the only two girls' schools to do so. Miss Beale happily agreed to appear in person before the Commission but Miss Buss was terrified. She need not have worried. Although she claimed later to have little recollection of the proceedings, her clear answers combined with her air of feminine frailty won her many influential friends among the Commissioners (two of them, the Reverend Dr A. W. Thorold, vicar of St Pancras and later Bishop of Winchester, and

Dr J. Storrar later became Governors) and the Commission's final report owed much to her contribution.

In passing, it might be mentioned that it was during the Schools Inquiry Commission that Miss Buss devised the word 'Head Mistress'. For too long, she felt, the leading women teachers had been differentiated from their male colleagues by the use of terms such as 'Principal' or 'Superintendent'. While many were led to believe otherwise, Miss Buss always believed in parity between the sexes. And so the Ladies' Principal of 1850 became the Head Mistress of 1865.

The Commission found that the North London Collegiate School was exceptional in an otherwise mediocre educational environment for girls. It reported with initial understatement that 'the state of Middle-Class Female Education is, on the whole, unfavourable.' It found few schools that catered for middle-class girls but in most of those which did the Commission found 'want of thoroughness and foundation; want of system; slovenliness and showy superficiality; inattention to rudiments; undue time given to accomplishments and these not taught intelligently or in any scientific manner; want of organisation.' It confirmed the continuing existence of parental indifference to girls' education and of the view that girls were both less capable and less in need of an education similar to their brothers. And it revealed that almost nothing had been devoted to the education of girls from the many charitable endowments in existence. Compared with 820 endowed schools for boys, only twelve existed for girls.

Such a Commission, however, made up entirely of men, had its limitations in assessing middle-class girls' education and proposing the means for its improvement. The Commission reported that it found that women teachers in general seemed 'to shrink from the labour and responsibility of large schools' which in any case lacked the small-scale atmosphere reminiscent of home life which small schools could offer. And while the Commission agreed with Miss Buss that day schools were preferable to boarding schools, it saw nothing wrong in educating daughters as 'decorative, modest, marriageable beings.'

Such views were commonplace at the time. *The Imperial Review* considered that 'Home and home only' was the 'True College' for girls. *Echoes from the Clubs* in March 1869 went further: 'If the destiny of a woman is to be the companion of man and a mother of children, there is no need that she should educate herself into a state of energetic acuteness which might fit her for being the attorney of the neighbouring village or the pushing secretary of a joint-stock company.'

But the report did lead to the Endowed Schools Act of 1869 which specified that there had to be an annual examination of every school unless pupils were taking approved public examinations or were being inspected by the Board of Education. In addition, the Act was responsible for

A North London Collegiate School Certificate of Merit, awarded to Eliza Bell in 1859.

21

creating some eighty endowed girls' schools by the end of the century through the reorganisation of ancient charities and the reallocation of part of their income for this purpose. Furthermore, the curriculum established for many of these schools by the Endowed Schools Commission, featuring English, history, geography, French, German, Latin, mathematics, some form of science, as well as instruction in domestic economy and the laws of health, owed a lot to the nature of the education already being pursued at the North London Collegiate School and set a pattern for the best part of the next century.

From the Endowed Schools Act came the next stage in the School's evolution. Miss Buss wanted to secure the future of the School which was still in her private ownership. At the same time, she wanted to see it established as a great endowed public grammar school which would be linked with a completely new school providing a more elementary education for girls from poorer homes at much lower fees. This was an ambitious undertaking which would take ten years of struggle to achieve.

At the end of 1869 a public meeting was held in the St Pancras Vestry Hall which agreed to form a trust to take over the ownership and running of the School. The name of the School was altered slightly so that it became the North London Collegiate School for Girls and the trust deed was signed on 26 July 1870. Among the new trustees were Frances Mary's brothers, Alfred and Septimus, and David Laing's successor at Holy Trinity, Charles Lee. Over the next few months several more trustees were appointed, including Dr Storrar and Dr Thorold. From the trustees a Governing Body of fourteen was appointed for both the North London Collegiate School and the new lower school.

Miss Buss ensured that several of these new trustees and governors were women. It was important for the Head Mistress and for the School that women should be represented on the Governing Body to provide the empathy so critical during these pioneering years. Secondly, the appointment of women expanded further their experience of public life and they themselves had the opportunity of learning much from such participation.

To make way for the new lower school, the North London Collegiate School moved to larger premises in 202 Camden Road. The Camden School for Girls, under Miss Elford, opened at 12 & 14 Camden Street in January 1871 and by May that year had 112 girls on the roll. Education for girls at the Camden School ended after they had taken the Cambridge Junior Local Examination at the age of 15 but some fathers, who could afford only to send one girl at a time to the more expensive North London Collegiate School, used Camden School as a preparatory school for their younger daughters. Over the years there was a steady flow of girls from one school to the other. Sara Burstall, an outstanding pupil who became the second head mistress of Manchester High School, was a case in point. She joined the Camden School in 1871, moving on to North London

Collegiate in 1874. She recalled of her education at the Camden School that 'they did such good work with us; with low fees, and no grants of course, and no endowment, the classes were large, and the staff limited. Some were only student teachers receiving training and an honorarium.'

Miss Buss's plans for the future envisaged raising money both by appeal and through securing endowments under the Endowed Schools Act to fund both schools properly and to build satisfactory new school buildings. The Camden School with its low fees was unable to put any money towards new buildings while the North London Collegiate School, although self-supporting, reinvested any surplus funds in improving teaching salaries. In 1870 the North London Collegiate School was already the largest school of its type in the country. Increased awareness of the value of proper education for girls made both schools increasingly attractive and numbers rose steadily. By 1876, 449 pupils attended North London Collegiate and 393 the Camden School. The issue of new buildings became critical.

The appeal began in the autumn of 1870 but raising the necessary funds proved to be disappointingly slow. There was a continuing reluctance to devote ancient endowments to girls' education even in instances where trustees were sympathetic to such aims. While £60,000 could be pledged in one evening towards a new boys' school in the City, a similar meeting in aid of the North London Collegiate and Camden Schools raised only hundreds. Miss Buss felt let down that even some of those women who had been expected to back the appeal provided little support. But in late 1870 a public meeting, chaired by Lord Lyttleton, raised hopes and a private meeting in February 1871 brought an introduction to several City Livery Companies, notably the Dyers' and Clothworkers'. The joint Prize Day for both schools that year was used to promote the endowment of girls' schools and every member of every Court of every Livery Company was invited to attend. But these efforts to cultivate influential contacts had little impact.

Miss Buss became depressed and felt overwhelmed by the work she was undertaking. Her health was already indifferent and the hard work and anxiety of the 1870s aged her considerably. She was away from home most days from early morning till late at night in her efforts to persuade those with influence to support the appeal. She felt her own reputation did the appeal no good since many people wrongly believed that she had made plenty of money over the years. In fact, she had always ploughed money back into the School and she was returning part of her salary to the School while the financial situation remained difficult.

As well as the hard work associated with the appeal, Miss Buss was also feeling worn out by her difficulties in coping with the Governing Body. For a woman used to having the final word for twenty years, it was an unfamiliar relationship. She found it hard to overcome her frustration at having to be accountable to the Governors. She described herself as 'a caged lion' but she did not help matters by acting on occasion without reference to the Governors. Decisiveness had always been a key part of her character and she chafed at any restraint. The first chairman, Dr Storrar, also found the relationship difficult. He was used to chairing committees 'where the word of the chairman was law' and he looked on the formation of the Trust as a new departure rather than as a continuation of a School already 20 years old with well-established traditions. He probably also found it strange to be a member of a Governing Body where women had equal status with men. Dorothea Beale wrote to Miss Buss sympathetically: 'No one knows how much of one's health and energy is lost to the school by the anxieties of getting those who do not understand the complicated machinery not to interfere with things with which the head alone ought to deal.'

One of the reasons for the formation of the Association of Head Mistresses by Miss Buss and other leading head mistresses in 1874 was to compare notes on how they were treated by their Governing Bodies. In September 1874 Miss Buss had written to a friend that the time had come 'to form an Association of Head Mistresses and hold occasional conferences in order to know what we ought to assert and what surrender.' The first meeting took place at Miss Buss's home in Myra Lodge where Miss Beale took the chair and others attending included Elizabeth Day, Miss Elford from the Camden School and head mistresses from several of the new High Schools. Miss Buss became the first President of the Association.

All the same, none of this should obscure the fact that Dr Storrar was both an experienced educationalist and a strong ally of Miss Buss who

Miss Buss with some of the staff and sixth form, 1877.

worked hard both in establishing the Trust in the first place and then in seeking endowments for the schools. (It should also be pointed out that Miss Buss fell out with his successor, Dr Thorold, on at least one occasion.)

The appeal gained considerable prestige when the Princess of Wales agreed on 15 November 1871 to become patron of the schools, but even royal patronage did little to boost funds. Because of the slow progress of the North London Collegiate appeal, Mrs Grey's Girls' Public Day Schools Company, whose High Schools for girls were based on the template of North London Collegiate, decided instead to raise funds on its formation in 1872 through the more certain method of interest-bearing debentures. This depressed Miss Buss even further: 'There can be no doubt that the new school movement is leaving us high and dry.' She knew neither of her schools could afford to raise money in the same way and her only hope now lay in the Endowed Schools Commission.

Then a partial saviour appeared in the form of one of the Governors, Miss Ewart, who offered both a loan of £3,000 and a gift of £1,000 to the appeal. This allowed the Governors to secure the site of a former furniture emporium in Sandall Road for the future development of both schools. Shortly afterwards, in May 1872, the Governors heard that the Brewers' Company had agreed to a request from the Endowed Schools Commission to fund the two schools through an allocation from the income of the educational bequest left to the Company in the seventeenth century by Richard Platt. This amounted to capital of £20,000 bearing annual interest of 3 per cent to be divided between the schools. The Company later also donated £20,000 towards the cost of building.

Before building work could go ahead, however, a new scheme of administration for the schools under the Endowed Schools Act had to be

The youngest form with Miss Fawcett, 1877.

25

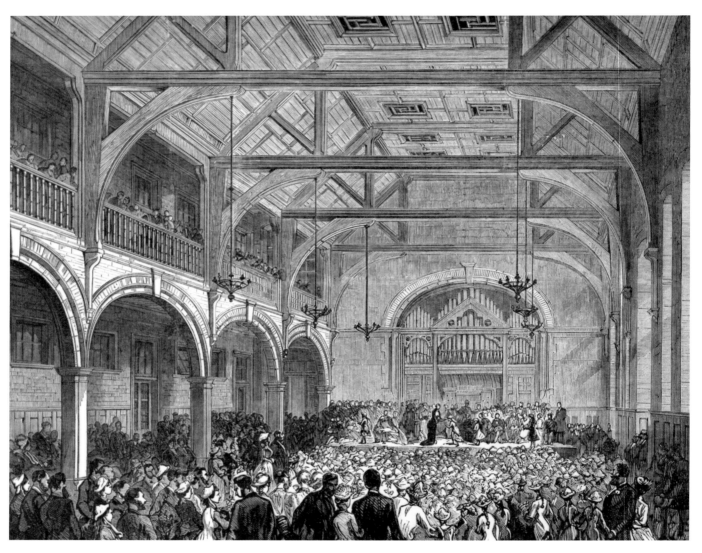

The Princess of Wales presenting prizes at the 1879 Prize Day in the Clothworkers' Hall

drawn up and approved. This was plagued by delays caused by the passage of the Endowed Schools Amendment Act and last minute objections and was not signed by the Queen in Council until 13 May 1875. The building programme itself was not straightforward. Originally the Governors proposed to house both schools on the site in Sandall Road. It was only at the suggestion of the Charity Commissioners (successors to the Endowed Schools Commission) in 1876 that plans were drawn up for buildings on two separate sites. A site was acquired in Prince of Wales Road, consisting of the house and garden which had belonged to the Governesses' Benevolent Institution, only for the Charity Commission to express concern at the cost of building on two sites, which the Governors had warned the Commission about in the first place! The Commission then proposed that the Camden School plans could go ahead so long as those for the North London Collegiate remained in abeyance. Both schemes were delayed while negotiations between the Governors and the Commission continued and it was not until April 1877, when the Brewers' Company offered to bridge the funding gap of £8,000 through a gift of £2,000 from Dame Alice Owen's charity and a loan of £6,000, that building work was able to proceed. At the same time, the Clothworkers' Company donated sufficient money to erect a splendid assembly hall, known as the Clothworkers' Hall, at Sandall Road. (The organ in the hall was funded by former pupils of the School.) The construction work on the Camden School buildings was interrupted by poor weather and strikes and on the North London Collegiate building by a dispute over the ownership of the freehold but these were minor problems by comparison.

While this major campaign was being waged, Miss Buss still had a school to run. The curriculum flourished and was praised for its breadth by the inspection team from London University which visited the School in 1876. The introduction of elementary physics, practical chemistry and botany strengthened the School's reputation for science teaching. French conversation classes were started while outside the classroom girls were sent swimming at the open air St Pancras Baths from the summer of 1872 (although one rule insisted that no girl should be in the water for longer than a quarter of an hour in case she caught a chill).

Prize Day reports featured lengthy lists of academic successes. By 1873 the School had sufficient examination entrants to establish itself as an examination centre for the Cambridge Local Examinations. No other

Girton College was founded by Emily Davies in 1869 in Hitchin. The College moved to its present site in Cambridge in 1873 and is photographed here in the early 1900s.

The North Londoners who passed the University of London General Examination for Women in 1877.

school in the country had either sent up as many candidates for the Senior Locals or had as great a success rate. Given the battle fought to achieve the same status for girls as for boys in these examinations, the emphasis placed on results was hardly surprising. But this did not necessarily mean that the School was an academic forcing ground. For example, Philip Magnus, the eminent educationalist who had headed the inspection team in 1876, reported that the aim of both schools was 'not to bring out certain pupils but to obtain good average attainments in each class'.

More and more academic opportunities were opening up for girls during the 1870s. Oxford University admitted girls to its local examinations. The Maria Grey Training College for teachers was established in 1871. Emily Davies established Girton College and Eliza Baker was the first Old North Londoner to gain an entrance scholarship there in 1872. (Three other ladies' Oxbridge colleges were founded in the 1870s – Newnham at Cambridge, and Lady Margaret Hall and Somerville at Oxford – but did not share Girton's ethos that there should be no difference between the higher education of men and women. For that reason, no girls from North London Collegiate were ever sent there.) The Convocation of London University, with Dr Storrar in the chair, approved the motion proposed by Septimus Buss for the admission of women to take degrees which finally occurred in 1878. These opportunities also allowed Miss Buss to begin recruiting talented graduates such as Rosie Aitken who taught classics and Sophie Bryant who taught mathematics.

Miss Buss, however, was by no means concerned for academic achievement alone. Thus, in 1872, for example, courses were held at the School in the philosophy of business, dress and food; and bookkeeping became a regular subject. The cookery class introduced in 1876 proved to be very popular with thirty-one of the thirty-two in the class gaining examination certificates.

By the same token, Miss Buss wanted to establish new job opportunities for her girls. In 1870 she corresponded with the Society for Promoting the Employment of Women. She attacked the Government in 1875 for restricting its office clerkships to men and praised the Post Office in the following year for enabling girls to sit examinations for vacancies.

The Camden School buildings were opened unofficially on 7 May 1878. Next came the grand opening of the Clothworkers' Hall on 18 July by the Princess of Wales who, accompanied by the Prince of Wales, also presented the prizes to both schools. For Miss Buss this occasion marked the School's coming of age. Now that the Clothworkers' Hall provided a large enough space for ceremonies to be held in the School, she decided that Foundation Day on 4 April should henceforth 'always be a day of importance in the year'.

The buildings of the North London Collegiate School were officially opened by the Archbishop of York on 29 June 1880. In his speech he pointed out that 'now it was almost universally acknowledged that women needed an excellent education in order to enable them to fulfil their duties as wives and mothers.' These views echoed those of Earl Granville who had told those gathered for Prize Day in 1878 that 'he could not believe that a sound, religious, moral and intellectual education would prevent a woman from doing her duty as daughter, wife or mother.' While Miss Buss would have applauded these sentiments from such eminent representatives of the Establishment, she would no doubt have noted the absence of any reference to the rights of women to use their education to earn a living. That battle was still to be won.

North London Collegiate School buildings in Sandall Road in 1890 – the School's 'third home'.

2

'A School . . . Yet in the Making'
1880–1910

The School is a great school, and every member of it appears to be quietly proud of her membership and happy in her place in it.

Board of Education: Report of Inspection 26–29 May 1903.

With the creation of the Trust and the opening of splendid new buildings, much praised in the educational press for their design and layout, Frances Mary Buss could concentrate mainly on the further development of the North London Collegiate School.

Sara Burstall later recorded of her Head Mistress that 'There was nothing narrow, or cold, or meagre about her! Imperious will, leader's instinct, mother-heart – all were hers and made her what she was.' As well as the Governing Body, many girls also experienced Miss Buss's 'imperious will'. Lilian Murray, who left the School in 1889 and in 1895 became the first woman to qualify as a dentist, felt that Miss Buss's autocratic attitude often created a feeling of resentment. She spoke from personal experience. Miss Buss had tried to persuade her to take up a career as a teacher of the deaf and dumb, which Lilian resisted in the face of increasing pressure from her head mistress. When Lilian exclaimed that she really wanted to become a dentist, Miss Buss, despite her genuine support for new careers for women, gave her no support or encouragement at all. Miss Buss, of course, was enthusiastic in her response to Lilian's achievement but by then the damage had been done.

Hester Armstead, later a member of staff, had a similar experience. Hester had been taught German by her governess before attending the School and her mother, herself taught by Miss Buss, had refused to have her wasting her time learning the rudiments of the language which she already knew. Mrs Armstead insisted to Miss Buss that Hester be placed in a higher class for German. Miss Buss refused in the irritatingly patronising tone she employed from time to time towards those she considered should know better. But she had met her match in the resolute Mrs

Facing page: *the greenhouse at Sandall Road in 1910.*

31

Armstead. Hester's sister, Lottie, later recalled that 'Miss Buss, tossing her head, took her [Mrs Armstead] to the class-room where Hester was listening to the German lesson and introducing her to the teacher made the ominous remark "Mrs Armstead thinks Hester can do higher work so I am trying her in the upper class. I *hope* she may not have to return here."' Hester did not have to return, Miss Buss acknowledged that Mrs Armstead had been right and in fact later invited her to join the Governing Body, recognising in her a woman of equal resolution and sympathy.

This streak of autocracy was unsurprising in one so single-minded but Miss Buss's maternal instincts were a more accurate reflection of her character. She had a wonderful empathy for both boys and girls. A much-loved aunt, she was given the nickname of 'Arnie' by her nephews and nieces. Alice Stoneham, who studied at the School until 1890, said that she 'never had any fear of [Miss Buss], from the day when, as a child of nine, taught only by governesses, I sat for the Entrance exam and received a motherly hug and kiss.' Smothering hugs from Miss Buss were experienced by many pupils during the early years of the School but as numbers grew so this side of their Head Mistress became more remote from the girls. In later years it was perhaps mainly the boarders who saw most clearly Miss Buss's warmth and generosity of spirit. She strove hard to make them feel at home. At Myra Lodge, the house in King Henry's Road, Regent's Park, which acted for many years both as her home and as a boarding house for a number of day pupils, Miss Buss organised Christmas parties and ensured girls had their own private space in the bedrooms by hanging curtains to create partitions.

She wore herself out by cramming so much into her hectic life. Her breadth of vision marked her out from many of her contemporaries, even from Miss Beale, and from many of those who came after her. For Frances Mary Buss, North London Collegiate was never the centre of the universe. She served on the Councils of the Cheltenham Ladies' College, the Church

Below: *the Sandall Road buildings in 1933; below right: the Clothworkers' Hall, photographed in 1890.*

The cast of the staff play, 1888, and programmes for two of the girls' productions: The Love of Alcestis *in 1883 (below) and* The Faerie Queene *in 1885 (bottom).*

Schools Company, the Maria Grey Training College, the Cambridge Training College, the Royal Drawing College and the Women's Branch of the Swanley Horticultural College; she was a Governor of University College, London, Milton Mount College, Aberdare Hall, West Ham Girls' School, the Grey Coat School, Westminster, and the London School of Medicine; and so the list of her commitments continued.

She made things worse for herself because her desire to bring about change was also accompanied by what Sophie Bryant called her 'talent for details quite extraordinary'. Many people assumed she had enormous resources of energy but her physical strength was never great. She was often overwhelmed by nervous exhaustion. 'It is simply sickening to think of the crowds who come to me,' she once wrote. 'I do my best to keep in health but overstrained nature will have her way sometimes.' On another occasion, writing to her brother, she remarked that 'You can never know the bitter price one pays for success. I think it is as heavy as that of failure.' Exhaustion brought out the worst in her, as it would in most people, and she grew old before her time. When Molly Thomas entered the School in 1883, Miss Buss was only 56 years old but Molly described her as 'a little white-haired old woman'.

Yet work was not everything to this remarkably active woman. Her social life was equally busy, with dinners and lunches, visits to the theatre and attendance at lectures, staying with friends in London, Cheltenham or Cambridge. She was quite happy to leave all her concerns behind once term ended and her holidays began. She applied as much energy to her holidays as she did to her term-time work. She loved new places and new

A scroll dated 1899, entitled 'Organization of Work', outlining the curriculum to be taught to each year group in the School.

people and was a convivial companion who never talked shop. She could laugh at herself – Lottie Armstead remembered her quoting the famous lines, 'Miss Buss and Miss Beale / Cupid's darts do not feel; / How different from us, / Miss Beale and Miss Buss!' with much amusement and appreciation. She would return from travelling quite relaxed, 'so elastic was her physique once the nerve strain had been shut off'. Her holiday memories often formed the subjects of lectures to the girls. In the spring of 1883, for example, she talked to them about the Riviera; in November 1886 Denmark formed the topic of her talk.

More usually her talks to the girls, given regularly every week, took a moral tone. According to Molly Thomas, they were rarely dull and every now and again Miss Buss delivered a comic lecture full of good jokes. These lectures, some of which were published after her death, are revealing about their author's character. 'Cheerfulness,' she believed, 'lengthens life; it makes all around us happy; it bears up against misfortunes.' She extolled happiness: 'I believe in happiness. I am sure our God meant us for it; I think we are the better for it; I long that every one of you should be happy in the fullest sense.' Courtesy, she pointed out, helped to smooth one's path in life. All these qualities were part of Miss

Prize Day, 1900 – the Jubilee year of the Frances Mary Buss schools. The function was attended by the Prince and Princess of Wales.

Buss's own personality. How much less resilient might she have been without her cheerfulness, without the delight she took in the world around her? How much less successful might she have been in a man's world without her natural courtesy?

These lectures were part of Miss Buss's aim of instilling within the School an ethos which could be passed on from generation to generation. The creation of traditions such as this was important in a young school. Even at Prize Day in 1907 William Latham, later chairman of the Governing Body, could refer to 'a School . . . yet in the making' which needed the sustenance of tradition. As well as ethos, annual school events were important in establishing a tradition of corporate life. Amongst the most important of these was Foundation Day. After 1879 this took over from Prize Day as the main occasion in the school year, an opportunity for the entire School not only to reflect upon the importance and meaning of its roots but also to open its doors to parents and friends from the outside world. Although reflective, it was not a sombre event: Molly Thomas considered it 'the merriest and most care-free day of the year'. In 1882, for example, it involved readings, songs and an organ recital; in 1890, a popular lecture was followed by an entertainment, given to the girls in the morning and to Old North Londoners and friends in the afternoon.

On both occasions, the gymnasium hosted an exhibition of toys and dolls made by the girls for distribution to local charities. A feminine ethic of charity was encouraged in a variety of other ways. Clothes for the needy were produced at the monthly meetings of the Dorcas Society. Girls took an interest in the Kyrle Society which sought to brighten up the lives of the poor by providing flowers and encouraging the use of flower boxes. The cookery class made Christmas puddings for the elderly.

The exhibition would become a regular feature of Foundation Day. Friends and former pupils sent flowers and evergreens to decorate the hall, of which the most distinctive was the daffodil, adopted by the School in 1883 as its emblematic flower. It was a pragmatic choice: in springtime they were plentiful, cheap and easy to obtain. (The school colours followed in 1892, selected as a symbol of the progress made in opening up education to women, with dark blue for Oxford, light blue for Cambridge and, according to the School magazine, orange for the new universities, and therefore as hope for the future. Today the colours are dark blue, light blue, and yellow.)

Prize Day was a much more formal and impressive occasion which highlighted the academic successes made by girls both inside and outside the School. For Miss Buss, Prize Day was an important means of communicating the success of the School to a wider audience. In pursuit of this, she knew the value to the School of securing the attendance of a person of influence or status. In 1883, Princess Mary, the Duchess of Teck, once again distributed the prizes (her first visit had been in 1873). For a

A classroom at Sandall Road decorated with daffodils for Foundation Day c.1890. The daffodil was adopted as the School's emblematic flower in 1883.

fortnight in advance, prizewinners were drilled in how to curtsy and walk backwards gracefully, with Miss Buss taking the part of the Duchess. Other guests in Miss Buss's time included Emily Davies, the founder of Girton, and the Secretary of the Endowed Schools Commission.

Tradition was more than outward show. The defining characteristic of the School remained a complete absence of class jealousy and distinction, something which the High Schools of the Girls' Public Day School Trust sought to emulate. This was taken so much for granted by the girls that it was almost unheard of for one to enquire of another what her father did. One girl reflected in later life that 'The difference in their religious faith and in their political creeds, the social differences between one girl and another – none of this made the slightest difference in their school standing.' Another remembered that there was never any sneering at Jewish girls at the School, 'only great interest in their Passover cake'. When inspectors from the Board of Education visited the School in 1910 they found that 'When once the surface prejudices had been overcome, the fusion of class strata was found to be not only a possible but a naturally helpful process.'

Miss Buss needed all the fortification her personality and the tradition of the School could afford during the 1870s and 1880s as girls' education came under renewed attack. In 1874 an article by Professor Maudsley based on scientific evidence available at the time summed up medical opinion which believed that the stress of female education endangered their ability to bear children. Mrs Lynn Linton, a fierce critic of liberal trends in girls' education, was not alone in her sentiments when she wrote in 1883 that 'a public and professional life for women is incompatible with the discharge of their highest duties or the cultivation of their noblest qualities.' In such a climate, those who were seeking to educate girls exactly so that they could follow a public and professional life could proceed only cautiously for fear of putting off prospective fathers. H. J. Roby, a former Endowed Schools Commissioner who spoke at Prize Day in 1884, was in a minority when he listed among the advantages of a girls' education their preparation to take up a profession and make their independent way in the world. The argument that an academic curriculum would turn girls into pedants unfit for a life of domesticity was apparently supported by research which discovered that in general girls' brains were several ounces lighter than those of boys. From this, it was argued that women should not seek to rival men in intellectual matters. Miss Beale remarked in 1888 that 'I was always hearing that girls would be turned into boys by studying the same subjects.'

Within the School, the arguments of opponents were derided. One writer in the School magazine in November 1883 commented on the 'nonsensical talk in the newspapers about the evil effects of High School education for girls: how it quite unfits them for domestic life, leaves them no time to study household matters, and, above all, to use their needles.' Yet even in 1909 girls and staff had to listen to a male defence of girls' education couched only in terms of its benefits to them as wives: the Bishop of Bristol told them at Prize Day that 'Women were not unsexed by their scholastic attainments; on the contrary, they were rendered better help-meets than they had been formerly.'

Miss Buss was in a better position than most of the head mistresses of the new girls' schools now opening up and down the country. She had developed North London Collegiate with success despite antipathy from many towards her aims and despite allies in the male establishment whose support was rarely wholehearted. Of all these head mistresses, she knew best how to reconcile her objective of providing an education as a preparation for life in its fullest sense with the femininity emphasised by supporters and opponents alike. So, while Miss Buss was horrified at Molly Thomas's inability to make a button-hole when she entered the School, she could also tell Molly's brother that, if she did not rescue his sister, Molly would be condemned to 'the dreadful career of stopping at home and helping mother – dusting the drawing room, arranging the flowers and other horrors.' This view did not contradict her belief in the importance of home as an influence upon character and personality but she saw the lives of all her pupils as having potential which reached beyond domestic boundaries. So in her weekly talks she urged all those who were leaving without going on to higher education to continue to cultivate their education with whatever means at their disposal; but insisted that each girl 'must take up all necessary domestic duties . . . she has to remember that there is domestic work for duty; work for necessity – to earn a living; as well as work for pleasure.' She could pour scorn on 'the follies of fashion. We ridicule savages because they put rings into their noses and lips, as well as their ears, and because they tattoo themselves; but is this more absurd than wearing tight dresses, high heels, and monstrous crinolines'; while impressing upon girls the value of work nearest at hand, in the home, for proving 'our energy, our firmness, our tenacity of purpose'. Ultimately, this was a rounded view of education for girls, reached after many years of experience, and it produced at the North London Collegiate School an all-embracing education which never jettisoned subjects simply to ape the boys' schools as occurred too frequently at many other girls' schools of a later foundation.

To preserve this compromise between femininity and progress, Miss Buss placed a premium on discipline. She preached self-control because she knew from personal experience that it had often been her failure to maintain self-control under pressure which had led to conflict in her career. Her own weakness was one reason which led her to create a complex system of discipline at North London Collegiate. Another must surely have been that she had had to fight hard to achieve as much as she had on behalf of her sex; this struggle dictated that her own pupils should be disciplined and driven. This almost became an obsession and during the 1880s it seems to have got out of hand. Rules were prescribed to cover almost every eventuality; in later years Sara Burstall wrote that 'as new misdemeanours arose, new rules were made to deal with them.' Girls were expected on their honour to enter their offences into the 'Appearing Book', appending their signature to each offence. The accumulated number of offences appeared in the termly report. Too many signatures earned an imposition and the ultimate sanction was a summons to the Head Mistress's study where girls were often reduced to tears. Those forms which (very rarely) succeeded in lasting half-a-term without any entries in the 'Book' earned a free half-hour, known as a 'Gratification'. That such a short period of free time should be so highly prized illustrates in itself the degree of supervision imposed upon the girls. Molly Thomas found it all too much: 'We were forbidden to get wet on the way to school, to walk more than three in a row, to drop a pencil box, leave a book at home, hang a boot-bag by only one loop, run down the stairs, speak in class.' Some girls lived in a state of permanent anxiety, wondering with every minor transgression whether or not it ought to be entered in the 'Book'. All this obscured the fact that some rules had a purpose, such as the printed homework time-tables to be filled in and signed by parents, intended to ensure girls did not suffer from overwork and to reassure parents. Yet if a rule was challenged, Miss Buss's reply was 'multiply the results', the logical conclusion of which seemed to elude her. Molly Thomas wrote that Miss Buss's 'sleep must often have been broken by the nightmare of five hundred girls all running amok at once.' Molly Thomas was not unusual in her criticism. Her contemporary, Lizzie Benger, later head mistress of Swansea High School, remarked that while she was not bothered by the rules, some of her friends found them burdensome. Sara Burstall, both pupil and mistress

Sophie Bryant with the sixth form, 1900.

at the School, who had strict views herself on many issues, nevertheless found that rigid discipline was 'a real hindrance to intellectual life and to progress of thought and individuality of character'.

Prefects appeared for the first time in 1881, elected from members of the sixth form by their peers and members of staff. Their powers were limited but their influence was important in maintaining the tone of the School. Miss Buss generally enjoyed a close relationship with her prefects who could count among their privileges the freedom to speak anywhere at any time. Each form also elected two monitors from amongst its members.

The majority of girls passing through North London Collegiate experienced only this type of suffocating discipline. The minority who stayed on into the sixth form, including Molly Thomas, discovered things were markedly different. The sixth form, under Mrs Bryant, provided a breath of fresh air for the older girls. A much more relaxed atmosphere prevailed and a much closer and more mature relationship existed between teachers and taught. There were no rules and the girls could talk during lessons as they sat at comfortable chairs and tables in the School library which acted as their classroom.

Health and physical exercise was another area where a careful balance had to be struck between the requirements of a progressive education, concerns over the stress such an education might inflict upon girls, and the preservation of femininity. Since mortality rates among the young were high in any case, adolescent health was a common source of anxiety for Victorian parents. Death did not strike frequently amongst the girls of the North London Collegiate School (only six pupils died between 1880 and 1896, for example), partly because the School did its best to monitor the health of the girls. In 1881, the girls' exercises in the gymnasium came under the supervision of a lady doctor, Mrs Hoggan. She obviously felt that callisthenics were doing little to develop the girls' physiques. To establish whether or not this was the case, medical inspections were

Above left: *girls on the 'giant stride' apparatus in the gymnasium, 1882.*
Above: *a gymnastics display in the Clothworkers' Hall, 1900.*

started in 1882 with accurate medical records being kept from 1884. As a result, callisthenics gave way to gymnastics as a more effective way of developing the often stunted physique of some girls. In 1888 Miss Buss, concerned at the frequency of epidemics, initiated school health certificates for the first time.

Personally, Miss Buss had little patience with the more extreme affectations of femininity. One commonly practised at the time was the fashion for women to pretend to faint under stress or emotion. At the North London Collegiate School, Miss Buss would not hesitate to use a jug of cold water to bring a girl 'round', although more often than not the mere threat brought about an immediate revival. On one occasion Miss Buss was in church with a pewful of girls: 'I noticed that one of them looked like fainting. I leant across to her, shook my fist at her and said: "You *dare* faint." And she didn't.' The School also sought to liberate girls from the restrictions imposed upon them by the fashions of the day. Mrs Hoggan found in the early 1880s that many girls were wearing their corsets too tightly, with a difference of as much as an inch and a half between their unconstricted and constricted waist measurements. Mrs Bryant in particular led a campaign to persuade girls to give up their corsets. In 1889 an athletic trial of strength was staged between sixteen girls who wore corsets and sixteen who did not. The results provided evidence for Mrs Bryant's case and she included the findings in an article for the *Women's Gazette* in which she wrote that 'stays, however loosely worn, are still stays; they substitute the rigid stay of a whale-boned body envelope for the natural and beautiful play of muscles, preserved in their strength and firmness by wholesome use.' In the same vein, games kit worn in 1892, consisting of 'loose blouses and short skirts only reaching just below the knee', gave girls complete freedom of action. Parents, however, could not be persuaded to allow their daughters to wear gym tunics for morning drill until 1898.

Initially most physical recreation at the School was confined to the gym or to weekly swimming lessons. This was still a period of experimentation. No one was sure about the most appropriate form of exercise for girls and there were still many middle-class people who believed that exercise could easily be harmful for girls. In this context, even the incorporation of a gymnasium within a girls' school was a radical new departure and, according to one member of staff, it was only through tea parties and tact that Miss Buss was able to persuade her parents of its value. In 1885, under the auspices of a new 'Games Club', the gym during lunch hour was full of girls playing 'classical nine-pins', battledore, shuttlecock and fives, while balls flew about in all directions. It was the girls themselves as much as the staff who seem to have taken the lead in increasing the exercise they took. In 1889, for example, the girls adopted a home-spun form of squash, using tennis rackets, tennis balls and the walls of the gym. Since the School was never divided into houses, competitions were carried on between forms although little thought appears to have been given to the unequal advantage enjoyed over the rest of the School by the sixth forms. The playground hosted inter-form rounders matches but the girls soon tired of these and once again it was the girls who formed and organised another Games Club in 1890 to promote other sporting activities.

The first athletics sports day which took place on 5 July 1890 was regarded as very daring and steps were taken to ensure that it attracted as little attention as possible. It was supposed to be held in a field close by Miss Buss's cottage at Boscombe near Epping Forest but because of rain the venue was moved instead to Epping town hall. The first swimming sports day occurred at Hornsey Road baths on 5 October 1895. Swimming was the first sport in which girls from North London Collegiate competed against pupils from other schools. The first inter-school swimming match happened on 11 July 1891 when two North London girls took on two girls from Notting Hill High School at Kensington public baths. In the same year the School's champions also challenged Notting Hill High School at tennis and Blackheath High School at fives.

One of the School's distinctive characteristics was that lessons were now confined only to the mornings. Ostensibly, this was another concession to conservative opinion, instituted to protect the girls from overwork. In fact, according to Sara Burstall, its primary intention was to protect the teaching staff from overwork by giving them free afternoons in which to carry out their marking and preparation. But having lessons only in the mornings also enabled girls to be free 'to pay calls with their mothers in the afternoon' and to devote time to learning their domestic duties within the home. That was certainly in line with Miss Buss's emphasis on the influence of the home within a girl's education.

But she believed above all in the importance of academic achievement for girls. The academic success of the School was one of the clearest ways in which the arguments of conservative critics could be rebuffed and the anxieties of parents could be assuaged. It also armed the School's pupils with the confidence and competence to go out into the world and challenge its old orthodoxies. It was unsurprising that Miss Buss's Prize Day reports should contain lengthy lists of the achievements made by pupils and former pupils.

The curriculum changed very little, remaining broad-based, with the exception of the addition of mathematics. Sophie Bryant, who joined the teaching staff (or 'governesses' as they were still described in the School prospectus) in 1875, was a brilliant mathematician and the subject flourished at North London Collegiate under her guidance. Miss Buss, of course, had taken some time to be persuaded that mathematics was suitable for girls and, while Miss Buss became a convert to the cause, this

A glowing school report, 1894, belonging to Rose Eveline Welch, and signed by Miss Buss and Sara Burstall, as form teacher.

The drawing school, Sandall Road.

Sophie Bryant, c.1895, at the end of the period in her career during which she was groomed as Miss Buss's heir apparent.

attitude lingered on for many years even among leading female educationalists. In the early 1870s, for example, the curriculum advocated by the Girls' Public Day School Trust still omitted mathematics. Sara Burstall, despite her strong connections with North London Collegiate and friendship with Sophie Bryant, believed that tuition in the subject should be kept at a minimum since mathematics was 'useless to them and disconnected with their life' and had 'a hardening effect on the nature of women'. The weaknesses in the School were art, although Miss Buss did introduce the examinations of the Royal Drawing Society, and music. From one overseas visit to Sweden in 1888, Miss Buss brought back the subject of 'slöjd', a form of elementary woodwork, which 'helps to raise the ideal of the dignity of manual work.'

Sophie Bryant and Sara Burstall were teachers of the highest calibre and they were not alone at North London Collegiate. Their employment reflected the results of Miss Buss's efforts to raise the status of teaching, to foster training and further the academic opportunities available to young women. With the eligibility of women to take degrees, there were nine graduates on the teaching staff by 1885, eight of whom were former pupils. By now, almost all the teaching in the School was done by women, something which would have been impossible ten years earlier.

Since she believed that teachers should be both highly educated and well trained, Miss Buss insisted that all new members of staff should have a certificate in teaching proficiency from either the College of Preceptors or Cambridge University. Training courses were also given within the School. She was a driving force behind the efforts which led to the creation of the Cambridge Training College in 1885 (this became part of the University Department of Education in 1949 as Hughes Hall, after the first principal). To get the College off the ground, Miss Buss paid the rent for a year on the cottages housing the first eleven students. Four of these were Old North Londoners, one of them being Molly Thomas. Sophie Bryant also travelled to the College each week to give lectures. Miss Buss told the Governors in June 1891 that 'the vast improvement in the quality of Girls' education which has taken place during the last fifteen years has been brought about mainly by the improved education of their teachers.' It was her view that her staff, as well as possessing 'University attainments equal to those of men', were 'also superior to the assistant-masters in the possession of knowledge as to the principles underlying their work and the methods by which these principles can be applied.' This was one of the most striking demonstrations of how Miss Buss's work had a positive effect upon education in general.

With others, Miss Buss was also instrumental in setting up the Teachers' Guild in 1883 with the purpose of transforming teaching into a profession. A local section was inaugurated with a soirée at the School in March 1889 for which more than a thousand invitations were issued. Academic attainments and training qualifications formed part of this transformation; another part was to ensure that salaries were paid which were appropriate for these new properly trained graduates. Sara Burstall recalled that she joined the staff in June 1882 at 'an exceedingly good salary, £120 per annum' and salaries were still reported to be 'on a liberal scale' in 1903. In 1890 the School instituted a savings scheme for teaching staff to boost their own personal savings with bonuses distributed among staff, weighted more heavily in favour of those on the lowest salaries. A pension scheme, involving Imperial Life Assurance, was introduced at North London Collegiate in 1897 and at Camden School in 1901.

As from the girls, Miss Buss insisted on strict discipline from her staff. An agreement dating from 1881 which had to be signed by each member of staff lists twenty rules, covering everything from keeping in order the register, schoolroom, lockers, furniture (for which there was a separate list!), and 'all things connected with my class' to ensuring ink was never used except for special examinations and was never left in the desks.

Otherwise Miss Buss never made excessive demands of her staff. She had always believed in fostering womanhood in its most complete sense. Just as she saw nothing wrong in combining a liberal education with the accomplishments which had traditionally defined femininity, so she saw no reason why her staff should have to jettison other characteristics of their sex simply because of their education and position. Fashion was a case in point. Miss Buss made sure that her wardrobe kept up with the pace of fashion. She wore well-tailored gowns, had 'a weakness for good lace' and strongly believed that all women should make the most of their appearance, especially those with 'advanced' views. Sara Burstall remembered that Miss Buss 'always insisted on the younger ones [of her staff] having pretty clothes, and set us a good example of dignity and taste in her own attire, and of splendour in her evening dress.'

Some head mistresses expected undying devotion to their school from staff and resented their departure upon marriage. This was the principal reason why women gave up teaching since convention decreed that married middle-class women did not work. (Widowhood provided an opportunity to return as in the case of Mrs Bryant.) But Miss Buss knew that there was more to life than lay within the boundaries of the North London Collegiate School, as her own wide-ranging external interests and love of travel and socialising demonstrated. While she had rejected several offers of marriage herself, she took no puritanical pride in this, unlike a number of other head mistresses. Instead, she looked upon these rejections with regret. As an essentially warm and loving personality, she took real pleasure in the marriages of members of her staff and in at least one case positively encouraged an engagement.

She wanted her staff as much as her pupils to think for themselves, insisting that they draw up their own plans for their lessons and

Sara Burstall, one of Sophie Bryant's brilliant contemporaries.

The staff, 1890. Miss Buss is seated in the second row, fourth from the right, and Mrs Bryant is on her left.

welcoming their participation at staff meetings in discussions on policy. She encouraged the most able to move on to headships of their own, a policy continued by her own successor as Head Mistress, Mrs Bryant. In 1898 Sara Burstall became head mistress of Manchester High School for Girls, one of the earliest of the new High Schools, founded in 1874, when three of the four candidates were Old North Londoners. It was Miss Buss who had sparked off Sara's ambition, giving her the opportunity of a wide variety of work as well as involvement with the professional associations, permitting her to write for the educational journals and supporting her successful application for a travelling scholarship to the United States in 1893. Several other members of staff successfully applied for headships during this period, including Miss Todd (Falmouth High School, 1897), Miss Gurney (Newcastle High School, 1902), Miss Young (Aske's School, Hatcham, 1907), Miss Bartram and Miss Hugon.

There were inevitably some members of staff who were weak. This was not, as Molly Thomas criticised, because the staff was drawn wholly from former pupils. Miss Buss appointed staff from outside the School throughout her career. Many of the assistant mistresses were Old North Londoners but this was scarcely surprising since the School provided a major source of female graduates. The endurance of weaker teachers at the School stemmed from a weakness of Miss Buss's own: rather than sacking those who were incapable, she 'wore herself out trying to make third-rate people do first-rate work.'

Molly Thomas voiced other criticisms of teaching at the School. Barely a word was spoken in French while any love she might have had for

Shakespeare was destroyed by the pedantic way in which it was taught. In general she felt that teaching at North London Collegiate was obsessed with accuracy rather than truth – 'Marks were the life-blood of the school' – and pursued a 'textbook-and-water' method which was mind-numbingly boring. Edith Allen, on the other hand, was a near-contemporary of Molly's and, while she experienced instances of an obsession with accuracy, found that 'Many mistakes may have been made but I think it [the School] was very good. We did not have too much learning by heart: poetry every day – English, French, German, Latin – I still remember German songs: first class botany, with myriads of specimens, and microscope work.'

Any criticisms there could be about teaching experienced lower down the School evaporated with admission into the sixth form. Sophie Bryant, who led the sixth form, was one of the shining stars of the teaching staff, gaining the nickname of 'Urania', the heavenly muse. Classics was the remit of Miss Armstead, brisk and vigorous with her lorgnette, a 'mental aristocrat' who 'gave the Collegiate touch that justified the title of the school.' The senior English mistress was Emily Hickey, an Irish poetess and friend of Browning, who co-founded the Browning Society in 1881. The botany so appreciated by Edith Allen was taught by Miss Davies, a beautiful and charming woman as well as a fascinating teacher. Sara Burstall was admired by her pupils, who called her 'the divine Sara', for the lively and invigorating way in which she taught history. The teaching of history appears to have been one of the School's strengths. One of Miss Burstall's colleagues was Miss Palmer, a disciplinarian and a partisan admirer of Cromwell and the puritans, 'with a supreme contempt for the Stuarts and all they stood for (the class took sides and History work benefited).'

There were long-serving staff like Miss Begbie, one of the first teachers at the School, 'a very large and motherly official', who retired in 1900 after serving for fifty years. And eccentrics, like Mrs Carr-Shaw, the mother of George Bernard Shaw, and singing mistress at the School between 1886 and 1906, whom one pupil could still picture in her mind's eye many years later at a Prize Day rehearsal 'wearing a bonnet with the ribbons untied and hanging down, and beating time with a short stick in her hand.' There still remained several male members of staff, including Septimus Buss, Mr Gray (writing), and the Reverend Mr James (composition) who used to refresh himself with sherry and biscuits.

This eclectic mixture produced excellent results, creating the academic success which satisfied parents and pacified critics. After an inspection of the School in 1887, the chief inspector wrote to Miss Buss that 'I have long considered your school – judged by results – as the best girls' school in England.' There was some criticism made that this did little for the majority who became wives and mothers but this was made in hindsight. The point has been made already that the North London Collegiate School sought to prepare all its pupils both academically and domestically. It was only a

Eleanor Begbie, one of the first teachers at the School, who retired in 1900 after fifty years' service.

Mrs Carr-Shaw, mother of George Bernard Shaw, and the eccentric singing mistress at the School 1886–1906.

minority of girls who joined the increasingly strong sixth form, the springboard for further academic achievement through university entrance.

The late nineteenth century was a period of real advancement in the academic opportunities available for women. The efforts of Miss Buss and other campaigners like Emily Davies, Maria Grey and Dorothea Beale had paid off. After London University had admitted women to degrees in 1878, a steady flow of other universities followed the same path. The new university in Ireland was one of the first in 1879, women were admitted to degrees in all the Scottish universities by 1892, Durham University opened its doors to women in all subjects except theology in 1895 and women gained entry to the University of Wales in 1900. At other universities, notably Oxford and Cambridge, there was continuing resistance to awarding degrees to women but here and elsewhere university courses were available to them and several new colleges for women were opened including St Hilda's and St Hugh's at Oxford and, in 1886, the Royal Holloway College in Egham.

In the summer of 1880, Clara Collet became the first Old North Londoner to achieve the degree of BA, gained at London University. In the following year and at the same university, Sophie Bryant and Florence Eves, an Old North Londoner, became the first women ever to be awarded the degree of BSc, both of them gaining first-class honours. By 1887, the 157 women who had graduated from London University included twenty Old North Londoners (the proportion remained much the same by 1900). Two pupils had also graduated from the Royal University of Ireland while twenty-nine had qualified for the Cambridge BA which was still not open to them.

Despite this progress, the occupations open to these women, particularly in the professions, remained limited, either by convention or deliberate decision of the professional bodies. Both branches of the law, for example, remained closed to women until after the First World War. By the late 1890s only a handful of women had qualified as engineers and it was 1899 before the first woman was admitted to the Institute of Electrical Engineers. Even in the medical profession, the growth in the numbers of women qualifying as doctors was slow, with only 264 registered in 1895. Teaching and nursing employed more educated women than all the other professions and even in these areas openings were available only for the most able. Nevertheless, in the face of these trends, middle-class attitudes were changing as families now expected their daughters to support themselves until they married. Clara Collet (who had become one of only four women to be appointed an assistant lady commissioner for the Royal Commission on the Employment of Women in 1892) was able to write in 1902 that 'the tendency among the girls themselves is to concentrate their energies on the profession they take up, and to regard marriage as a possibility which may some day call them away from the path they are pursuing, which should not be allowed to interfere with their plans in the meantime.'

Clara Collet, the first Old North Londoner to achieve a BA, awarded by London University.

Old North Londoners played their part in the teaching profession and in overseas missionary work, another favoured occupation for many women. But, graduates and non-graduates alike, they also pioneered many new career choices. The need to consolidate the success of the School may have compelled Miss Buss to emphasise the academic record of her pupils but in the long lists read out at Prize Days she never forgot to include those whose achievements were practical rather than academic. The practical elements in the curriculum were extended for leavers by providing courses aimed at future employment such as preparation for the civil service, technical education and dress-making 'on scientific principles'.

Girls from North London Collegiate forged careers in horticulture, pharmacy, dentistry, photography, interior decorating and furnishing. Margaret Buchanan won the Silver Medal of the Pharmaceutical Society in 1887 and her pupil, Doris Gregory, another Old North Londoner, later became the first woman to be awarded the Society's Fairfield Scholarship. (As Lady Jephcott, Doris Gregory later became one of the most generous of the School's benefactors.) Among the same generation as Lilian Murray, the first woman dentist, was scientist Agnes Robertson, who left in 1890 and became a Fellow of the Royal Society. Theodora Morton became an influential social worker and was the principal organiser of childcare work for the London County Council.

An outstanding pioneer was Marie Stopes who fought against all sorts of prejudice in her public promotion of birth control methods. She had shone in her early career as an academic scientist and in 1904 was the first woman to be appointed to a university staff when she became an assistant lecturer in botany at Owen's College, Manchester. Her schooldays had a great influence upon her life and she left instructions that only daffodils should be placed on her grave and that the School hymn, 'To be a Pilgrim', should be sung at her funeral.

Mention must also be made of the contribution to the fight for equal suffrage made by Old North Londoners, encouraged by the example of Miss Buss, Mrs Bryant and others who made no secret of their support for women's suffrage. Myra Sadd was typical of many in her membership of bodies like the Women's Freedom League, the Women's Social and Political Union, the Tax Resistance League and the Women's International Suffrage Alliance. Like a number of other Old North Londoners, she suffered a term of imprisonment and endured the torment of force-feeding for her beliefs.

As the nineteenth century drew to a close, it was suffrage which began to eclipse education as the major issue for activist women. Miss Buss would have regretted that. While a great deal had been achieved, she knew that much remained. Educational opportunities were still unequal for women. Until the educational playing field had been levelled, how was it possible for women to enjoy the same career freedom as men?

Marie Stopes, an outstanding pioneer for contraception and women's rights.

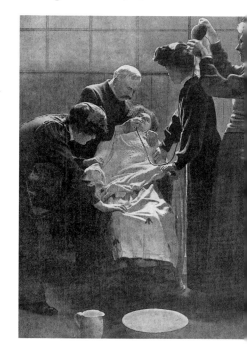

A suffragette being force-fed by means of a tube through her nose, 1912.

The huge contribution made by Frances Mary Buss to this fight had worn her out. She suffered badly from gout, kidney ailments and repeated attacks of the flu. She was absent from the School for most of the 1893–4 school year. She visited Sandall Road for the last time on 7 November 1894 to give out prizes for holiday work but fell seriously ill soon afterwards. Lapsing into a coma for three days, she died at the age of 67 on Christmas Eve. Her death was reported widely in national newspapers, an indication of how she was recognised during her own lifetime for the significance of her contribution towards education. Her funeral took place on New Year's Eve when more than 2,000 people filled Holy Trinity Church in Kentish Town where she had been a regular worshipper for so long. The names of the pall-bearers reflected Miss Buss's standing in the world of education: Emily Davies, Dorothea Beale, E. P. Hughes, the President of the Association of Head Mistresses, representatives from London University, the College of Preceptors, the London County Council, and Her Majesty's Inspectorate, as well as the Acting Head Mistress and Head Mistress of her own schools, Sophie Bryant and Fanny Lawford. A special train conveyed 600 mourners from Kentish Town for the burial at Theydon Bois.

In her honour the two schools became known collectively as the Frances Mary Buss Schools. A memorial window was presented by her family to Holy Trinity Church and another by the Clothworkers' Company to the North London Collegiate School. The sum of £2,000 was subscribed in her memory to establish a travelling scholarship for teachers, reflecting her love of travel and its beneficial effects and her work to raise standards within the occupation she had done so much to transform into a profession. At North London, Foundation Day became Founder's Day in 1895. On that occasion, white, not yellow, flowers were worn, the hall was not decorated and a concert of sacred music replaced the usual exuberant songs. When the memorial window given by the Clothworkers was

Just some of the many and lengthy obituaries of Miss Buss, demonstrating the high regard in which she was held, and the recognition of her outstanding work for women's education.

*Frances Mary Buss, 1827–94, founded
North London Collegiate School in 1850.*

*Sophie Bryant, 1850–1922, who
became Head Mistress in 1895.*

Two paintings by R. W. Buss (Frances Mary's father), which today hang in the Buss Library at Canons. The bottom picture, entitled 'The Court Martial', depicts a cat being tried at Waterloo for killing a canary. R. W. Buss is both judge and sentry, and the little girl is Frances Mary.

unveiled in January 1896, girls walked in procession to lay daffodils beneath it, a tradition which continues in altered form to this day in memory of the remarkable woman who founded the School.

The North London Collegiate School remains her living memorial but her contribution to education can still be seen in the profession to this day, from the equality of educational opportunity freely available to girls to the continuing emphasis placed upon both qualifications and training for new teachers.

Although Sophie Bryant was a brilliant scholar and teacher, she never considered leaving the School during the twenty years between joining the staff in 1875 and taking over as Head Mistress in 1895. She knew that she was being groomed as heir apparent. The Governors, however, insisted firstly on appointing her as Acting Head Mistress in January 1895, and then on advertising the post and carrying out interviews. The formal announcement of her appointment was made to the pupils by Alfred Buss, as Clerk to the Governors, on 10 July but the girls broke into spontaneous applause before he finished. On the last day of term, pupils and staff arranged a secret celebration for their new Head Mistress. At the final assembly, a specially composed song (which referred to Mrs Bryant as 'The mistress of the whole School's choice') was sung in her honour, three cheers were given and each of the prefects and monitors presented bunches of roses.

Sophie Bryant had been born Sophie Willock on 15 February 1850 at Sandymount, near Dublin. Her father, the Reverend W. A. Willock, was a fellow and tutor of Trinity College, Dublin. The third of six children, Sophie spent her formative years in Ireland and was educated at home as her father moved from Dublin to parishes in Cork and near Lough Erne. In 1863 the family settled in London where Dr Willock took up the position of professor of geometry at London University. Sophie, an intelligent and vivacious child, studied at Bedford College where she soon displayed her academic gifts. In 1866 she was awarded the Arnott Scholarship for Sciences and in the following year gained first-class honours in the senior division of the Cambridge Local Examinations. Two years later, Sophie's marriage to Dr William Hicks Bryant in Plymouth appeared to have brought any thoughts of an academic career to an end but her husband died only a year later.

As a widow, it was acceptable for Sophie to take up an occupation and she obtained a teaching post at a school for ladies in Highgate in 1870. Five years later she joined the North London Collegiate School as the mistress in charge of the sixth form. She was still only 25 years old but her talent was clearly evident to Miss Buss who pressed her to take her degree at London University. Not only was Sophie Bryant one of the first two women to graduate with a Bachelor of Science degree, she was also the first

Frances Mary Buss and Sophie Bryant in 1893. Below: the letter, written in 1878, in which Miss Buss strongly recommends that Sophie Bryant be her successor.

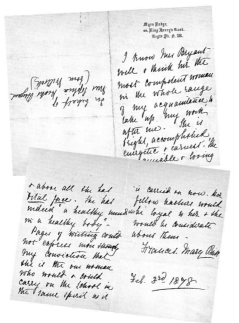

woman to obtain a Doctorate of Science at the same university in 1884, an achievement which gave Miss Buss and the whole School great pride.

She was exactly the kind of teacher Miss Buss was looking for. Miss Buss wrote of her in 1878 that 'she is bright, accomplished, energetic and earnest. She is amiable and loving and above all she has vital force.' Although she was not the clearest of teachers, Sophie inspired her pupils to work and think things out for themselves. Edith Allen recalled that when asked for advice, Mrs Bryant encouraged the questioner to reach their own conclusions based on reason and knowledge. Together with her Irish sense of humour and kindly sympathy, this created a close bond between sixth-form mistress and pupils.

Sophie Bryant had a very open personality and never hid her strong and passionate views on a variety of subjects. She had a long list of publications to her name totalling almost fifty, comprising books, pamphlets, articles and lectures on education, morality and ethics, religion, mathematics, philosophy and her beloved Ireland. She was a keen exponent of women's suffrage and while she declined to play a key role because of her other commitments she was an occasional platform speaker at rallies. She called herself a 'suffragist' rather than a 'suffragette' since she disliked the violent tactics of the latter. She was an ardent supporter of Home Rule and even persuaded Miss Buss to the cause (Sara Burstall, on the other hand, always felt Mrs Bryant's support for Home Rule was unwise in the interests of the School). There is one story about Mrs Bryant, Miss Buss and several others enjoying a fortnight's holiday in Ireland in the spring of 1885, the year prior to the introduction of the first Home Rule Bill. The party engaged in lively political discussion with other guests in the hotels they stayed at, something which Miss Buss would have enjoyed. Mrs Bryant often wore an orange scarf with her navy-blue dress; the author of an account in the School magazine remarked that 'it was quite delicious to think of an ardent nationalist like Mrs Bryant travelling about Ireland with the emblems of the opposite party aggressively displayed.' These emblems so disgusted the beggars along the road in one district that they forgot to beg from the band of passing travellers.

The School's Debating Society, begun by sixth formers at Mrs Bryant's suggestion in 1887, enabled her to give expression to some of her political views. The first debate on the justification of insurrections saw her sympathising with past disturbances in Ireland but considering a 'revolution' as unnecessary although she felt the converse would be true in Russia. The Society's second debate proposed that everyone should be given the vote while a debate in 1888 approved a motion proposing the replacement of the House of Lords by a 500-member body nominated by the House of Commons.

Mrs Bryant enjoyed physical as well as intellectual exercise. The same author of the account of the Irish visit noted 'the irresistible influence

50

Sketches that appeared with an article about North London Collegiate in The Lady, *4 June 1891.*

which everything in the shape of a mountain exercises over Mrs Bryant.' There are several photographs of her in skirt and soft hat atop crags and rocky outcrops and the hills and mountains she climbed included those of the Lake District, North Wales, France and Switzerland. She was an early cyclist, taking up the pastime in 1893 when it was still considered somewhat shocking for women.

She was already well respected in educational circles before she succeeded Miss Buss. Miss Buss had been invited to become a member of the Royal Commission on Secondary Education chaired by her great friend, Sir James Bryce. She had been too ill to take up the offer but in her place Sophie Bryant was appointed as one of the three women on the Commission, the others being Lady Frederick Cavendish from the Girls' Public Day School Company and Mrs Henry Sidgwick, the Mistress of Newnham College. The significance of the Commission lay in its recommendations for bringing control of the several types of secondary education under one central authority, a newly constituted Board of Education, formed in 1899, and at local level under education committees, created by legislation in 1902, of the county councils or boroughs.

Sophie Bryant was an advocate of the wider view of education promoted by Miss Buss. This contrasted with many of her peers who, although able in their own right, often tended to take a more parochial

Sophie Bryant (second from the right) on the pinnacles of Crib Goch in 1897.

view. By contrast Mrs Bryant had extensive external commitments during her headship. In 1898 she became the first woman to be elected by the Convocation of London University to the University Senate where she sat for seven years. She served on the Technical Education Board and its successor, the Education Committee of the London County Council, until 1910. In this forum, she supported scholarships to enable elementary school pupils to attend secondary schools and fought for the development in secondary schools of laboratory work and practical domestic economy. She represented the Technical Education Board on the London Polytechnic Council and became a member of the Consultative Committee of the Board of Education in 1900. In 1903–5 she presided over the Association of Head Mistresses. She was as enthusiastic a supporter of teacher training as Miss Buss. For twenty years she was a member of the Board of Studies of Pedagogy at London University. Her campaign for a London teacher training college and a chair of education at the university resulted in the appointment of a new professor in 1902 who simultaneously took charge of the London Day Training College. For many years Sophie Bryant herself chaired the Training College's Council. Similarly she was deeply involved with Goldsmiths' College after it was transferred by the Goldsmiths' Company as a training college to London University. She was also honorary director of the Henrietta Barnett School from its inception.

She believed in providing the broadest possible education for children. In her address to the Association of Head Mistresses in 1904 she said that 'We easily fail to realise the worldwide horizon of the child's natural desire for knowledge . . . In our concern about set lessons and definite acquisition, we are only too apt to forget the glorious, though somewhat incapable, versatility of the child, and thus to neglect the development of that interest in all the vast miscellaneous world, which is the prime universal requisite of intellectual education.' The curriculum at North London Collegiate was often criticised by inspectors for being too broad which meant that sometimes there was a rush, particularly in the lower school, to cram in the teaching needed to meet the requirements of the Cambridge Examination Board on any one subject. Mrs Bryant, rejecting any pressure from external exams as exaggerated, was sure in her response: 'Our plan of work provides for an all-round education in every case, neither Languages, Science, nor English culture being allowed to monopolise attention.'

Her emphasis was upon intellectual education: 'Sleepy senses must be awakened and blinking intellect trained to be open-eyed.' Her training as a mathematician gave her a strong belief in rigorous study and all girls were encouraged to tackle in part the more difficult subjects and to execute accurate scholarly work. In retrospect, one of her colleagues and her eventual successor, Miss Drummond, felt that Mrs Bryant's standards could be discouragingly high for some: 'To the best, the fare that she provided was sheer joy. Of others she sometimes asked more than they were capable of giving.' On the other hand, Mrs Bryant did recognise the limitations of some of her pupils, establishing what were known as technical forms for the study of home crafts and household business.

Like Miss Buss, she gave her staff the space and freedom to develop their own ideas. Sophie Bryant appreciated constructive criticism and welcomed free-ranging discussion at the continuing regular full staff meetings. Second mistresses were appointed only intermittently and by and large responsibilities were shared out among all the staff rather than being restricted to a few senior mistresses. Neither were there heads of departments. Instead there were individual subject committees comprising all the relevant staff where junior staff were expected to make a contribution.

Mrs Bryant maintained the generally high calibre of staff at the School. Inspectors in 1903 gave unanimous and high praise to the quality of the staff 'which for thorough efficiency could hardly be surpassed'. The

Sophie Bryant 'at home' in 1905.

inspectors continued that 'the freshness and vitality of the older members, whose energy custom has in no way abated, were particularly noticeable.' An example of newcomers to the teaching staff was Eleanor Doorly who joined in 1907. A trained graduate, as almost all the staff now were, her linguistic skills were outstanding. She read Ibsen in the original and learnt Russian so she might do the same with Dostoyevsky. The author of several books, she was remembered as 'a tremendous spur to the young' and went on to become head mistress of the King's High School, Warwick. Another was Charlotte MacRae who taught domestic science at the School from 1904 until 1929, a woman of rectitude and kindliness from whom many pupils learned their habits of thoroughness and pride in good work.

There were few weak subjects within the curriculum but music had been one of the weakest at the School since its foundation. Here the greatest improvements were made. These came from the appointment of Mrs Manson to succeed Mrs Carr-Shaw in 1906. Many members of staff were striking characters in their own right and Mrs Manson, who headed the music department until 1936, was one of them. She had been a pupil of the great violinist, Joachim, had known Brahms and had been taught singing by a pupil of Mendelssohn. The state of music in girls' schools, she later recalled, was 'Mendelssohn and water, mostly water; dreadful stuff'. She set about with gusto to change all that. She searched through the collection held by the British Museum for new music for the School choir to perform and in 1910 dusted off the cobwebs from Purcell's *Dido and Aeneas* which had not been performed since its première at a girls' boarding school in Chelsea in about 1689.

The performance caused a musical sensation. Professional musicians were brought in for the orchestra while young doctors from two local hospitals were recruited to the choir, although they had to be concealed by screens on the stage! Dido's role was taken by Christine McClure who sang beautifully while Marjorie Muir's performance as Aeneas was notable because it was the first time bare legs had appeared on stage at the School. The performance was well reviewed by *The Times* and heard by H. G. Wells who was overwhelmed by the music.

Mrs Manson knew Holst and Vaughan Williams, both of whom did much to raise the standard of music in schools. The School choir sang the former's *Rigveda* in the version for female voices. Holst had been intending to conduct the performance but arrived late. Overcome by the sound of the music being sung by young female voices (he had heard it sung only by the mature voices of the Manchester Choral Society), he was too moved to conduct. Mrs Manson also knew Charles Stanford and encouraged him to compile the *National Songbook*.

Sophie Bryant stamped her own impression upon the atmosphere at the School. A much more consistently relaxed personality than Miss Buss, and visibly so, she brought a greater freedom to the School which reflected its

One of the many paintings of the School crest, together with its explanation, that Septimus Buss regularly gave to pupils.

54

The Death of Dido – a scene from the 1910 production of Dido and Aeneas.

growing maturity. Many rules either disappeared or were relaxed. Eveline Short, who joined North London Collegiate from a boarding school in 1908, relished the School's relative freedom, the absence of petty rules and a standard of work and behaviour which was taken for granted.

Partly, this freedom was expressed through the development of games and other leisure activities at the School. A hockey club was established at one of the boarding houses in 1896, followed by a School club in February 1900. The problem was the lack of a suitable nearby playing field. Instead, a field at Highgate was shared by both North London Collegiate and Camden School. A playing field fund was opened in 1900 but it was not until 1909 that a suitable field was acquired on a long lease in Camden. A basketball team was started in 1906, using the gymnasium during the dinner hour.

A Science Club (with its separate sections for photography, geography and gardening) was formed while the Debating Society was amalgamated with the Literary Society in 1910 to establish the Social Discussion, Literary and Debating Society. There were the usual discussions and lectures (including one by Ernest Shackleton on his Polar expeditions) while one innovation was a mock general election held by the senior girls in 1910. A junior girl, Norah Horobin, later head mistress of Roedean, was so disappointed at being excluded from the vote that she organised a petition in protest which she presented to Mrs Bryant. The Head Mistress gravely told her that the petition was invalid since it had been headed 'Votes for Miners'. The Unionists secured a narrow victory. The School magazine noted that the election was 'carried out with all the proper formalities – in-so-far as the procedure inside a polling booth could be ascertained by those not yet allowed to enter one.'

The Dorcas Society continued its charitable efforts and was joined by the Missionary Society and the Sunshine League. A nurse's fund was set up in 1903 to support a parish nurse doing mission work in the parish of Holy Trinity in Kentish Town. The Sunshine League arranged meetings, lectures and fund-raising events, made slippers out of old felt hats and soft toys from scraps, and organised trips and parties for the less fortunate. The League's Christmas parties became legendary: 'in the days when poverty and strikes meant that our little guests were really thin and cold and often hungry, . . . Sandall Road seemed to them like fairyland.'

The School appeared to be strong and healthy and in many respects this was so. But what could not be overlooked was a flaw which had existed ever since Miss Buss had handed the School over to a Trust in 1870: a lack of finance. When an inspector, Mr Mitcheson, from London County Council visited the School and its sister, the Camden School for Girls, in 1899, two points in particular stood out from his report. Firstly, he noticed a decline in the neighbourhood. Secondly, he expressed his surprise that 'two such famous schools should have no endowment beyond buildings and repairs funds and certain Scholarships and Exhibitions', meaning that both Schools had to rely almost entirely upon fees for finance. The two points were connected as the School found to its cost. As Camden deteriorated, so numbers at the School fell; as numbers fell, so funds declined. In 1901, with its finances in debit, the School had to raise its fees. By the turn of the century, more pupils were coming to the School from farther away. Steadily increasing fees were becoming a hurdle for a number of them and entrance scholarships were suggested as a possible solution. By 1910, it was being noted that fees were already high enough and that the School's greatest need remained a regular annual income. Another effect of straitened finances was that teaching salaries at the School, which had once led the field, now began to fall behind those paid elsewhere. Whereas they had been 'on a liberal scale' in 1903, by 1910 they were in need of improvement.

There were other financial considerations. Both Schools were in need of expanded accommodation but how was this to be funded? Camden School, where lower fees had to meet similar costs, was struggling with inadequate buildings, excessively large class sizes (as many as fifty in some), poorly paid staff and hardly any money to make improvements in any of these areas. Here any rise in fees would have an even greater impact on numbers than at North London Collegiate. By 1906, Camden School was seriously overcrowded, cramming 366 pupils in a space fit for 250, and it was sustained only by good work, excellent discipline and grants from the London County Council. It was only the scholars and funds from the latter which had saved the School from closure but now overcrowding put at risk receipt of any further funding from the Council. Closure was discounted since it would have been 'a public disaster' but unsuccessful attempts were made by the Governors (who as Trustees of the Frances Mary Buss Foundation were Governors of both North London Collegiate and the Camden School) to sell the School to the County Council before an agreement was reached for the Council to fund the School through an annual maintenance grant.

When the Education Act of 1902 had been passed, the Governors had declined a grant from the Board of Education for North London Collegiate but parlous finances had brought about a change of mind in 1907. In 1904 North London Collegiate had also accepted funding from the London County Council in exchange for extending its allocation of places for LCC scholars to 10 per cent every year. (The School had first admitted scholars from elementary schools in 1894, the first important secondary school to do so.) The strong links which existed between both Schools and the London County Council made it natural for the former to seek some arrangement with these bodies which would provide greater financial security and enable the urgently needed building programmes to go ahead. In January 1908 the County Council, in exchange for increased representation on the Governing Bodies, pledged specific grants towards the building programmes. The Board of Education also provided additional grant aid towards the building costs with the Schools raising the balance through the issue of debenture stock.

This arrangement enabled Camden School to be provided with additional classrooms, a library and an extra playground. At the North London Collegiate School classrooms, staff rooms, a science room and a domestic arts room were added. The new buildings at both Schools were opened during 1908–9. In 1910, a new Trust scheme was approved for the Frances Mary Buss Foundation which increased the number of Governors to twenty-three, providing the London County Council with five places and the Middlesex County Council with three. A minimum seven places were prescribed for women.

With the immediate financial crisis settled, the inspection team from the Board of Education visiting North London Collegiate in 1910 could applaud the standard of improved accommodation. They could also remark that Mrs Bryant 'has made a lasting mark on the intellectual life and development of the School.'

The weathervane on the Bryant Wing, which was opened in 1909.

PRESIDENT
H·M·THE·QUEEN·

SCHOOL FROM CAMDEN ROAD

NORTH·LONDON
COLLEGIATE
SCHOOL for GIRLS
SANDALL Rd CAMDEN Rd NW

FRANCES MARY BUSS FOUNDATION 1850

School Enlarged and Educational facilities Extended in 1909

SPRING TERM BEGINS JAN 13 1910

FOR PROSPECTUS APPLY SECRETARY

Electric Cars pass the door

nr Hampstead Tube Railway

3

'Constant Change and Development'

1910–39

Do not be critical of changes as they come; they are the very essence of our tradition. It is because this School has always looked forward that it remains an ambitious and successful environment.

Prize Day Report, 1938.

The two principal observations made by the inspectors who reported on the School in 1903 dominated the development of North London Collegiate over the next thirty years. As the nature of Camden altered, with the middle classes moving further away from the centre of London, the School's catchment area widened and its composition altered. Although the School's sustained high standards persuaded many parents from the suburbs to send their daughters there, not enough did so, largely because of travel problems, to make up the difference created by those lost locally. Falling numbers reduced fee income which was in any case insufficient. A shortfall in funds continued to be the main obstacle to implementing any improvements at the School.

When inspectors from the Board of Education reported on the School again in 1914, they noted that 'the neighbourhood is on a downward grade.' Numbers had dropped from 480 girls in 1903 to 392 by 1910. In 1914, the School comprised 343 pupils aged from 8 to 18. The most acute fall seems to have been in the Junior School, ranging from 8 to 13 years of age, which had shrunk to twenty-five pupils as a direct result of the deterioration of the surrounding area. Mrs Bryant suggested the creation of a kindergarten for children under 8 years old as a way of trying to make up numbers and the Governors agreed in 1913 to open up the School to girls and boys from the age of 6, boys being admitted only until the age of 13. But this initiative attracted only handfuls of young children and made little difference to declining numbers.

Facing page: *an advertisment for the school displayed in Tube stations in 1910. It was designed by Mr Lee, the architect of the Bryant Wing, which was opened in 1909.*
Below: *Sports Day, 1912.*

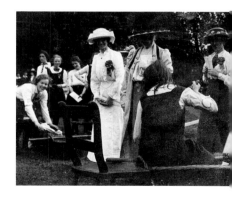

Form I in their classroom at Sandall Road, 1920.

The 1914 tennis team.

Even the sixth form was shrinking, down from forty-five in 1911 to twenty-nine in 1914. For all her protestations at Prize Days, Mrs Bryant was unable to persuade more girls to stay on at school beyond the fifth form. This was in spite of the sixth form's excellent examination record. In 1911, for example, forty-one out of forty-six girls matriculated, thirty-six of them with distinction. In that year eighteen girls went on from the School to university while in 1914 twenty-three out of twenty-nine sixth-form leavers took up university places.

It was the Middle School which, according to the inspectors, was the engine-room of North London Collegiate, blending together existing pupils, scholars placed by the London and Middlesex County Councils and a large number of girls from more distant locations attracted by the School's reputation. The School had taken the decision in October 1913 to increase the number of free places it offered each year from 10 per cent to 25 per cent so that it could qualify for the new additional annual grant of £1 per pupil being introduced by the Board of Education. By the end of 1914, nearly a third of the School consisted of LCC scholars.

The change in Camden, combined with a growing influx of girls from the suburbs, was altering the social composition of the School. In 1910, 35 per cent of pupils came from professional families, wholesale and retail traders accounted for 34 per cent of girls, and another 25 per cent came from families where fathers were clerks, commercial agents or artisans. A quarter of all girls came from within the county of Middlesex. Only four years later, professional families accounted for 46 per cent of pupils, wholesale and professional traders 28 per cent and clerks, commercial agents and artisans 17 per cent. It seems likely that it was only the admission of scholars with free places which prevented an even greater change.

Higher fees do not appear to have been a factor in this shift. At an average of £20 9s. 6d. a year in 1914, they were the same as they had been in 1910. They were still insufficient for the School to dispense with grants from the Board of Education. Fees and grants together remained inadequate to pay proper staff salaries. (They would have been even worse had pay scales not been revised by the Governors in 1912.) The inspectors pointed out in 1914 that average teaching salaries at North London Collegiate had now fallen behind those at the Camden School while salaries at both Schools were lower than the scale recommended by the local education authorities.

All these problems were overshadowed by the coming of the First World War. The public imagination was caught by the plight of Belgian civilians during the early months of the conflict and North London Collegiate welcomed several Belgian refugees, adding a few Russians later in the war. The girls were soon knitting vigorously for servicemen and refugees. For example, by the end of 1914, Belgian orphan babies seeking refuge in Holland had been sent fifteen pairs of knitted shoes, fifteen vests, four jackets, twelve bonnets, six flannels, four nightgowns, two diapers, two bodices, one binder, and two mufflers. This continued until wool became scarce towards the end of the war. The Sunshine League collected old clothes for East End children whose families had been thrown out of work because of wartime changes. Working parties were created to sew for the local military hospitals. Between 1915 and 1917, a number of forms each adopted a prisoner-of-war held in Germany and sent them fortnightly parcels. Letters sent by return from these prisoners were often read out in assembly by Mrs Bryant (who herself chaired the Irishwomen's Association for Aid to Irish Soldiers in the War). In May 1916 a party was

The cast of the staff play, 1917.

Below: *Camden High Street in 1907.*

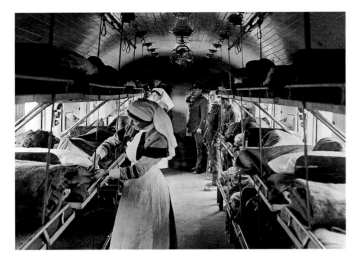

Above: *a nurse on a British Ambulance Train near Doullens in 1918.*
Above right: *V. A. D. motor ambulance drivers at Etaples, 1917.*

given for seventy-five wounded soldiers at the School, the School magazine noting that 'The conversation was at first rather strained but the atmosphere warmed before long.' Sports prizes and choir prizes were sacrificed in favour of making donations to war funds. A regular financial commitment of 30s. a week was made by the girls to support two beds for wounded soldiers in the Great Northern Hospital. The Jewish girls in the School collected money for the relief of Polish Jewish refugees.

The full horrors of the war brought home to so many boys' schools by the loss of recent leavers made little impression at North London Collegiate. Few women had any experience of the front line although many Old North Londoners did valuable work as nurses and doctors. Often, however, they participated through the voluntary organisations, like the Red Cross or the Voluntary Aid Detachment, whose amateur approach was resented by trained nurses. Some attempt was made to convey the sacrifices being made by recording from time to time in the School magazine the deaths of brothers, cousins and friends. Ten days after the armistice came on 11 November 1918, a thanksgiving service for both Foundation Schools was held at Holy Trinity Church, led by the Bishop of Stepney.

By now Mrs Bryant had retired. She had given notice to the Governors during 1917 that she wished to step down at the end of the 1917–18 school year. After giving forty-three years of her life to the School, Mrs Bryant felt that the time had come for a fresh face to take the helm and tackle the unresolved problems left over from before the war. She enjoyed her retirement to the full but only four more years were given to her. On a walking holiday near Chamonix in the summer of 1922, she slipped and fell, spraining her ankle. After bathing her foot in a stream, she lay down in a state of shock, passed into unconsciousness and died. Her body was found a day later and she lies buried in Chamonix.

Facing page: *a press cutting from 19 August 1922, before Sophie Bryant's body was found in the Alps.*

The third Head Mistress of the North London Collegiate School was Isabella Drummond. Born in Hampstead in 1877, she was the youngest of nine children. Her father, Dr James Drummond, was the principal of a training college of intending Unitarian ministers. Isabella was educated at one of the new high schools, Oxford High School, and, studying from home, took first-class honours in natural sciences at Oxford. She taught at Loughborough and Edgbaston High Schools before joining the staff at North London Collegiate in 1908. Six years later she became Head Mistress of the Camden School for Girls. Although her term there lasted only four years, she quickly put her own stamp on the place. When she applied for the headship at North London Collegiate, one of her referees, Cloudesley Brereton, a schools inspector with the London County Council, summed up her contribution to the Camden School. With girls 'whose docility had become somewhat excessive', no doubt because of the rule-bound regime of the time, she had increased their self-reliance and enterprise. The standard of work had improved as a result and she had persuaded more girls to stay for longer. Within the School she had created 'an atmosphere of briskness and vitality'. Her skills as an organiser were praised as were her qualities of tact and discretion, judgement and insight, enthusiasm and initiative, firmness and sympathy. Brereton concluded of her that 'she is at once both conservative and progressive.'

She was an inspiring teacher. Mary Sutton was taught botany in the sixth form by Miss Drummond whom she described as 'the best teacher I have ever met'. A tiny figure with a deep voice, she combined, as a Head Mistress, the distance yet warmth so typical of many of her peers. Her presence would bring immediate silence. Those who did not know her could find her aloof, cold and unapproachable; yet laughter was often to be found in her company. Even-tempered and blessed with a sense of proportion, she never minded silence and cared little for small talk but she was a good listener who enjoyed a funny story. Never profuse in thanks or appreciation, her few words therefore meant much more. She was well liked by the girls. When her niece, Ruth Drummond, a pupil at the School, told one girl in response to a question that she was indeed Miss Drummond's niece, the questioner responded 'Lucky pig!'. Another Old North Londoner recalled that Miss Drummond was 'gentle, caring and considerate', a 'calm, efficient and serene' Head Mistress, who ran the School with 'clarity, firmness and compassion'.

Mrs Bryant told her successor to remember that schools were growing and living things which had to change and develop. Isabella Drummond had no trouble with this sentiment. It concurred with her own beliefs. She stressed the North London tradition of 'constant change and development' as part of 'a continuity of personality' where continuity was given by 'the overlapping of generations'. Looking back on Miss Drummond's headship, one former pupil reflected on the almost imperceptible way in which change was introduced without destroying traditional values.

Isabella Drummond in the Head Mistress' Room, 1920.

Below: *Isabella Drummond with the Science VIth in 1913.* Below right: *the botany lab, 1922.*

The freedom she had created at the Camden School she instilled at the North London Collegiate. Reducing rules to a minimum stimulated a livelier atmosphere and promoted greater self-reliance and intellectual enterprise. She had no time for the concept of a prefect as a policeman, believing in leadership by example. So while the prefects had almost no sanctions to impose, she delegated to them most of the responsibilities for running the School outside teaching hours, creating in the process closer links between them and the staff. Other rules remained, including the homework slips regulating time spent on homework which had to be signed by a girl's parent.

Miss Drummond quickly won the confidence of her staff. She maintained the system of subject committees inherited from her predecessor and encouraged her staff to develop their own subjects within the framework of the syllabus. Although always available to them, she urged them to use their own initiative and made it known that she had little time for trivia. The ability to delegate she had shown in relation to the prefects she displayed also in relation to her staff, distributing responsibilities widely among them. Regular staff meetings discussed general educational issues as well as internal matters which had 'the advantage . . . of giving effect to ideas introduced by fresh young members of staff and of keeping all members in sympathy with new developments.' One innovation was her introduction in 1919 of a 'Grace Term', a sabbatical for members of staff with more than seven years of continuous service. Another was her persuasion of the Governors in 1925 to pay for supply teachers in the event of staff absences, something which had been hitherto the responsibility of the staff member concerned.

Miss Drummond had a knack for making good appointments. Caroline Senator was a remarkable teacher of French, German and Spanish at the School from 1919 to 1958. Inspiring and scholarly (she came top of her

Hockey and netball in 1922.

year in French at London University), Miss Senator's brightest pupils regularly won Open and State Scholarships while the weakest made steady improvement. One of her many pupils later recorded that 'her teaching of literature [was] an experience of a uniquely educative and thrilling kind' and she created 'a sense of worlds to be conquered that were just beyond one's present reach and that it would be sad indeed to miss for want of trying.' Edith Cross joined the School in 1920 to teach geography, having been educated at the School and taken a B.Litt. at Oxford. A firm disciplinarian as well as a gifted teacher, she also became the School's devoted archivist. Edith Hodgkinson, known as 'Hodg', started teaching English at the School in 1921, remaining for fifteen years. She brought with her an infectious love of literature: 'She was at her best with the most able and least able pupils, stretching the minds of the former, whom she was incapable of cramming, gently encouraging and sustaining the latter. Some of the "middle" group found her lack of instruction disconcerting.' The English department also included Miss Gibbons, who died in harness in 1932. Helen Gardner, later Dame Helen Gardner, professor of English literature at Oxford, was the ablest of her pupils, writing that Miss Gibbons 'made her lessons an adventure which she shared with us . . . No pupil of hers could ever forget that the end of poetry is delight and our study with her was that we might enjoy more fully.' The report of the Board of Education on the School in 1937 is illustrative of the overall calibre of the staff during this period. Geography was taught by 'very good teachers'; those teaching science were 'well-qualified and experienced'; in history classes there was an 'atmosphere of friendly discussion between teacher and taught'; scripture was taught with 'freshness and sincerity.'

Isabella Drummond believed that education was for the many, not the few, and that the most important work of the School was 'the guiding of an individual . . . to a sound perception of the values on which to base

Dame Helen Gardner, professor of English Literature at Oxford University, whose love of the subject was kindled at North London.

The Science VIth, 1922, at 62 Camden Square, where they took observations for the Air Ministry, so as not to break seventy years' records of rainfall – just the kind of enterprising project encouraged by Miss Drummond.

her life.' She had no intention of allowing academic standards to slip, believing that a secondary school must be a place of 'sound scholarship', but that there also had to be a place for the 'ordinary' person. 'School,' she said, 'is as much concerned with sending into industry, commerce, home life or hospitals, girls with trained intelligence, initiative and a sound sense of the true values of life as it is with helping those who should proceed to specialised intellectual work to obtain entrance to the right place for higher education.' She told her pupils that those among them who persisted even without striking success could obtain as much satisfaction as those ostensibly more successful provided that they found their own niche: 'It is worth much trouble on the part of both school and home to help a girl to find her own special gifts and tastes and the line of work where she will be able to use these to the best advantage.'

She was in fact espousing careers advice and advocating a policy in advance of her time. This was important since in the years immediately after the First World War the advances made by women during the war diminished as men returned from the forces to their old jobs. By 1921, women were once again confined to the same limited number of occupations, which for middle-class women largely meant teaching. This was further exacerbated by economic recession and unemployment which reinforced a tendency to prefer men to women in senior positions. This was in spite of the fact that the status of women was benefiting from post-war legislation. Partial suffrage came in 1918, followed by equal voting rights in 1928. Women were granted equal rights of divorce in 1923 and of guardianship in 1926, the year in which their pension rights were also increased. The Sex Disqualification (Removal) Act 1919 enabled women

The chemistry lab, 1920.

to be allowed to 'assume or carry on any civil profession or vocation' although nothing was said about equal pay (the pay of women teachers, for example, was regulated at 20 per cent below that of male teachers). The problem for many women was that marriage still continued to bar them from a number of occupations. The civil service would not employ married women; wives could not be nurses; women teachers were still required to resign their posts by their wedding day, a barrier which was not removed until the 1944 Education Act. In July 1921 one Old North Londoner, Dr Gladys Miall Smith, refused to resign from her post as a medical officer on the occasion of her marriage. Her dismissal by her employers, St Pancras Borough Council, caused a furore.

Miss Drummond was perpetuating the School tradition of urging its pupils to go out and push back the boundaries in a male-dominated world. She told girls in 1926 that they should seek 'the less well trodden ways' rather than drift into clerical work as an easy option. Although the Head Mistress perhaps placed more emphasis than her predecessors on the future of the less academically inclined, this too was very much in keeping with the traditions of the School. It was also in contrast to the trend in girls' schools during the inter-war period to shape the curriculum around university entrance, often modelled increasingly on boys' schools, with scant regard for the needs of the less able.

Miss Drummond's belief that the nature of the curriculum should be led by the needs of the individual made her a critic of the examination system, the oppressive effects of which some were beginning to question during the 1920s and 1930s: 'Examinations are a fence which must be jumped before entry into most professions [but] parents, I think, are in the main in agreement with me that examinations must as far as possible be taken by the way and not made an end in themselves, and I think there is a growing recognition of this point of view among the girls as well.' Miss Strudwick, the High Mistress of St Paul's, was another who deplored the fact that the School Certificate was now only regarded as a qualification for university entrance. Sara Burstall disliked the burdens being created by the demands of the system which she believed restricted the ability of teachers to do what they believed to be in the best interests of those they taught.

Miss Drummond believed that there was no uniform pace at which girls developed and that the requirements of each pupil should never be lost among the many. So, for example, she created a 'loop year' in the fourth year for the benefit of girls younger than their age group. She had a particular interest in girls deemed disruptive by others whom she preferred to consider as difficult and wanted to retain within the School.

She actively encouraged a boom in new societies within the School as a means of broadening the extracurricular interests of the girls. When this threatened to get out of hand and absorb too much of the pupils' time the system was reformed during 1926. The number of societies was reduced

Ishbel MacDonald presenting prizes at Prize Day, 13 October 1930. Seated on the right, looking at the camera, is her father, Ramsay MacDonald, who sent both his daughters to the School.

Top: *young mothers in Bromley, 1921;* middle and bottom: *the opening of Frances Mary Buss House in 1927.*

to six, covering art, drama, music, gardening, literature and history, and photography, although restrictions on new societies appear to have been lifted in the 1930s, when the Chess Club, League of Nations Union and Current Affairs Society all appeared. No girl was permitted to join more than two. All of them were run by the girls and they provided opportunities for trips out of school or the invitation of renowned speakers. In 1924, for example, the Gardening Club took its members to Kew while the Photographic Club visited the British Empire Exhibition at Wembley. Among guest speakers appearing before these societies were Walter de la Mare, G. K. Chesterton, Laurence Housman, C. V. Wedgwood, Laurence Binyon and Arthur Bryant. Ramsay MacDonald lectured on socialism at the School in the summer of 1924, the School magazine reporting that while his 'moustaches . . . were not as long as we were led to believe by the cartoons' nevertheless 'many of us are now budding young Socialists.' MacDonald, who was Prime Minister at the time he gave his lecture, sent both his daughters to North London Collegiate. He also attended Prize Day in 1925 and returned again in 1930 to give the address, his elder daughter, Ishbel, an Old North Londoner, presenting the prizes. During her father's time as Prime Minister, Ishbel hosted a reception at No. 10 Downing Street to raise funds on behalf of the School for the Frances Mary Buss House.

Another notable Prize Day speaker was Sir William Beveridge in 1928 while in the previous year the Astronomer Royal, Sir Frank Dyson, whose wife was a former pupil, had been invited during the summer to talk about 'the event of the term'. That was the first total eclipse of the sun to be seen in Britain since 1724. On 27 June 1927 200 girls took the opportunity to travel by train to see the total eclipse at Richmond in Yorkshire. They were disappointed. At the crucial moment the sun disappeared behind a cloud. In referring to the enjoyment the girls had had from their visit, Miss Drummond asked at Prize Day: 'What will be the experience of the School in 1999? Perhaps . . . they will charter a fleet of aeroplanes and view the eclipse from above the clouds and so make sure of the corona. Being North Londoners, they must be enterprising.'

The School was not only able to attract illustrious speakers. When Queen Alexandra died in 1925, the School was also able to continue a tradition of royal patrons. The Duchess of York, later Queen Elizabeth, the Queen Mother, accepted the invitation to become patron of the School in 1926, relinquishing the position in 1937 after her husband became George VI. The School was delighted that the Duchess of Gloucester agreed to become the next incumbent.

The ethos of charitable and social work at the School continued to be fostered and the Sunshine League carried out work in Bromley-by-Bow, organising parties for the children of Aldenham Street School. From this came a deeper interest in the problems of children living in this poor area of the East End of London which was described as 'drab and dreary to the last degree, with no open spaces, no wide roads, nothing but evil-smelling factories to break the monotony of the rows of small two-storey houses.' (Such poverty was often to be found closer at hand. A friend of Ethel Howie was a scholarship girl too ashamed of the poverty of her home to invite Ethel inside her house. For the family of another scholarship girl, Maureen van Horn, the expense of new textbooks or new uniforms strained their limited finances to the utmost.) In 1919 two Old North Londoners, the Wordley sisters, opened a small house in the country at Witley which took in mothers and children from Bromley and gave them a holiday. (These operations later moved to a bungalow at Tankerton-on-Sea.) Two years later the School appointed Bertha Nicholls as a full-time social worker in the area, running clubs and liaising with other organisations. By 1926, the Old North Londoners Association was looking for a permanent base to house three girls' clubs and six children's clubs. The establishment of such centres was not new; Cheltenham Ladies' College had opened premises for social work in the East End before the turn of the century.

Fund-raising activities for the new centre, which it was intended to call 'Frances Mary Buss House' included a 'Great Fair' held in November 1926 which yielded £920. A former dairy was purchased for £1,475 which came with two large cowsheds, a garage and courtyard. Conversion provided a common room, kitchen, caretaker's bedroom, clubroom and a small flat for the social worker; the larger cowshed became an assembly hall, the pony stables a billiard room, the loft a library and reading room and the smaller cowshed a kitchen for teaching cookery. (An additional wing, named after Miss Drummond, was opened in 1937.) A number of parents were becoming more and more interested in the project and this led to the creation of the Parents' Guild, an association which still flourishes today.

Frances Mary Buss House was opened on Saturday, 8 October 1927. Three existing clubs were amalgamated into two, one for those between 14 and 16 and one for those over 16. The older girls would entertain the Mothers' Club once a month. An extensive programme of weekly activities was arranged, from painting, knitting and singing to folk dancing, handicrafts and games, and the clubs were also open on Sundays for Bible study. 'The great aim of the House was to make the girls feel that it belonged to them, and they to it; it was to be a place where they would always find sympathy and friendship.'

Although originally intended to cater only for girls, a boys' club was also formed, known as the 'Buss Rovers'. The activities of the House had created a respectful curiosity in the area within a short time of its opening. 'Buss Rovers' came about through the leader of a gang of small boys 'who had entered on a career of crime – who smashed windows and rang front-

Top: *a trip to Rookwood House, c. 1930;* middle: *washing up at one of the many Frances Mary Buss House camps, 1934;* bottom: *another camp, 1930.*

The library at Sandall Road, 1922.

door bells – and who yet swore to Miss Carré [the new social worker] by his mighty football team that the Frances Mary Buss House should be left unmolested – if he could rely on being admitted to it one day.'

To provide time for these activities, the traditional system of morning lessons was continued and Miss Drummond believed that 'the freshness and vigour' to be found in work carried out in the sixth form was due 'in large measure from the restriction of lessons to morning hours and the mixture of compulsory and voluntary activities.' (There was time for a mid-morning break where apples and cakes, at a penny each, or biscuits, at three for a penny, were available with one-third of a pint bottles of milk in the gymnasium.)

She was under no illusion about the disadvantages of this system but she believed these were far outweighed by the advantages: 'The shorter hours of teaching, the width of the curriculum and the opportunities given for optional classes all have their effect in lowering the standard reached in a subject for which a girl has little ability; but I believe that the fact she is given the opportunity to find some line of real interest, to throw a good deal of energy into this, and to achieve some measure of success, more than compensates for the slightly lower standards in the less congenial subject.' The curriculum at the North London Collegiate School remained a great deal broader than the often arid curricula found at some High Schools at this time.

The School's curriculum was strengthened for the most able by the introduction of advanced courses in science and maths, modern studies

Eirlys Jones taking a Junior School lesson in 1933, in the garden on the south side of the Bryant Wing.

The drawing school with Miss Monkhouse, 1930.

and classics, although the latter was short-lived. Miss Drummond also complained that the way in which grants for these courses were awarded by the Board of Education tended to restrict unduly the choice and combination of subjects. Art, for many years a neglected subject, benefited from the introduction of an advanced art class whose aim was to prepare girls for the Royal College of Art and the Slade. Miss Monkhouse, the art teacher, was a talented woman, the daughter of the art critic and minor pre-Raphaelite artist Cosimo Monkhouse.

Miss Drummond was eager to eliminate once and for all surviving notions that there were subjects beyond the average girl. In particular, she wanted to dispel a notion which must have grown up within the School during Mrs Bryant's time that 'mathematics was a difficult subject which only the really clever girls could do.' The School's fifth-form examination performance in the General School Certificate showed that many of those below the top form could still expect to achieve excellent results. By the early 1930s greater numbers enabled the introduction of broader courses, such as a general science course, tailored to the needs of those not destined for university but intending to pursue careers in nursing, physical education, domestic science teaching or household administration. The School succeeded in persuading more girls to stay on in the sixth form even if only for one year. This was a considerable achievement when as late as 1938 only four in every hundred girls nationwide were staying at school until the age of 17.

The results of striving to provide an education which tried to cater for the needs of all pupils was that leavers from North London Collegiate were as likely to be heading for a City office as for Oxbridge. In 1925–6, for example, thirty-six of the 120 leavers took up business and secretarial courses while others found work as milliners, librarians, gardeners and so on. Among girls breaking fresh ground in employment in 1935 were Molly Quennell (aeronautical engineer), Christine Vernon (chartered surveyor) and Coralie Sparks (veterinary surgeon). In 1938, twenty-two sixth-form leavers were taking up university places, six of them to Oxford or Cambridge colleges. Of the remaining thirty senior leavers, the most popular destination was secretarial work but the list included medical and dentistry schools, teaching, business, dressmaking, journalism and the civil service. Among the fifty fifth-form leavers, eight were heading for college, nine for secretarial work or courses, and ten for clerical employment, with the others distributed among hairdressing, millinery, physical education, nursery teaching, business, the civil service and chiropody.

Old North Londoners were also making their mark in the world outside work. They were being elected as councillors and serving as justices of the peace. Ermyntrude Harvey was a member of the British tennis team which won the Wightman Cup in 1926 and 1928. Eva Taylor was appointed professor of geology at Birkbeck College in 1930 and Gladys Milnes as professor of French language and literature at Bedford College in 1934. Joyce Reynolds edited *Harper's Bazaar* and Alice Head *Good Housekeeping*. Stella Gibbons achieved fame as the author of *Cold Comfort Farm* and a string of other novels. She was in the same form as Helen Gardner and Stevie Smith, one of the best poets of her generation.

The School's immediate environment continued to decline after the First World War: 'No thought or care could lessen the noise of the stream of motor transport which now passed up and down the Camden Road, nor diminish the dust and dirt which came in through the windows . . . Girls no longer lived in the houses around the School; they came in crowded trains from distant suburbs, and Camden Road seemed airless and shut in.' Most of these suburban travellers came from places in Middlesex such as Hendon, Wood Green, Finchley and Willesden. By 1926, while there were 175 London County Council scholars compared with nineteen from Middlesex, 222 fee-paying pupils came from Middlesex, outstripping the 155 from the London County Council area. In total, 330 pupils came from the LCC and 241 from Middlesex. Of the Middlesex contingent, 160 girls were making journeys each way of forty-five minutes or more, usually at rush hour, usually having to stand and often in anxiety of being late.

For many girls, Sandall Road was remembered by its evocative mixture of aromas, 'floor polish from the parquet, pungent apples from the store room, and school-lunch being prepared in the kitchens'. But buildings

Facing page: *the School at Sandall Road, painted by John J. Lee, May 1910.*

were no longer adequate and accommodation came under pressure from the post-war surge in numbers. From 390 pupils in September 1918, itself an improvement over pre-war figures, numbers rose to 510 over the next twelve months. By 1925, there were nearly 600 pupils, the School having opened with 450. North London Collegiate was full and applications were being turned down. The only additional building work was a new gymnasium in 1924. The only extra income came from the closure and sale of the boarding house, the proceeds of which were intended to be used to enhance opportunities for physical exercise by acquiring a larger playing field at Burnt Oak.

The Board of Education inspectors reported in 1926 that numbers were placing 'a great strain on accommodation' and noted that 'the present site is so restricted' and that 'freedom is hampered in many ways.' In submitting the report to the Governors, the inspectors sent a covering letter wondering whether the School on its present site could retain its numbers given that more and more girls were being drawn from outside the London County Council boundaries: 'If the present tendency becomes more pronounced it may force the conclusion that the School ought to be moved to a site more in the heart of its population.' The chairman, Dr (later Sir) Henry Brackenbury, pointed out the three main disadvantages of this idea: heavy building costs; the impact on grant aid from the Board of Education which any loss in the number of scholars from the LCC would have; and the disposal of the existing buildings.

Money was a major worry. When the Burnham salary scales were introduced for the teaching profession in 1920, the only way salaries at North London Collegiate could initially be brought in line was by raising fees from £6 16s. 6d. per term to £8 per term. It proved difficult to persuade the Board of Education of the case, prompting the Governors to record that 'The Board are probably well aware of the objections entertained by Governing Bodies of schools of this type to accepting the restraints and hindrance incidental to the receipt of funds from the local authority, and the very real interference thereby occasioned with the elasticity and adaptability in the organisation and methods of schools which are characteristic of English education at its best.' But increased fees (they were raised again to £10 a term in 1921) were insufficient to cover the full implementation of Burnham for which the School had to seek further assistance from the London and Middlesex County Councils. The Governors tried but failed to persuade the LCC to provide funds without the usual strings attached but this was rejected. The consequence of these strings became apparent during 1923 when public spending was being cut back. A reduction of 5 per cent in salaries was urged upon all schools, whether they were maintained or voluntary aided, and North London Collegiate risked the wrath of the Board of Education if it did not comply. (In 1931, when the economy was in even worse shape, the Governors implemented without

Facing page: strolling along the herbaceous borders in the grounds of Canons, 1990s.

hesitation another series of cuts in staff salaries even though the recommendations for such action from the LCC did not actually apply to the School.) With virtually no money of its own, the School was reliant on bodies like the Board of Education, the London County Council and the Middlesex County Council. It seemed very unlikely that a move to a new site could be funded without their support.

Perhaps Miss Drummond had been thinking already about a move. In any case, she was very receptive to the suggestion made by the Board of Education inspectors. The more she thought about it, the more she concluded that it was the right thing to do, regardless of any problems that might have to be overcome. Before the Governors had even considered whether or not the School should move, she took it upon herself to persuade them by finding an appropriate site. The Underground had just been extended to Edgware, then still surrounded by fields, so one day during the autumn half-term of 1926 Miss Drummond with two other members of staff, Miss Odell and Miss Monkhouse, decided to explore the area. It was here that they discovered Canons.

Miss Odell later wrote to Miss Cross that 'It was a lovely day and we walked for miles through flat fields without being in the least allured. Then we found ourselves in Edgware Road and came to the Canons drive with its large notice of sites for sale. So we went up it. You remember how lovely it was when it was quite untouched, and the autumn colouring was very good that year, so we were entranced. On the left presently a sunny field sloped away to the southward, and we said "What about that?" and went on. By great good luck some repairs were in progress so the gate

Canons, engraved by Woolnoth, from a drawing by J. P. Neale.

was open and we went to the house, and on to the South Terrace. The view was looking its very best. I said "Think of turning the children out here at lunch-time!" At the time it seemed completely impossible.'

Miss Drummond knew that she had found the perfect site. She arranged to meet Dr Brackenbury and reminded him of the inspectors' recommendation. 'You didn't take that seriously, did you?' he asked her to which she answered that she took it very seriously. She asked him to take a look at the property. He too returned quite convinced.

Canons, in the different spelling of Cannons, was the name given to the great palace built in the early years of the eighteenth century by James Brydges, the first Duke of Chandos, out of the profits earned from his post as Paymaster of the Queen's Forces Abroad. No expense was spared on either the house or the grounds. James Gibbs was the principal architect; Belucci, Sir James Thornhill and Grinling Gibbons were among the artists and master craftsmen employed; and William Kent was consulted on the layout of the gardens and grounds. The Duke and his family moved into the uncompleted house in 1714. The Duke kept his own orchestra and in 1717 he asked Handel to conduct it. At Canons Handel wrote the series of anthems now known as the Chandos Anthems. Here too in 1719 the first performance of the cantata *Acis and Galatea* was given on the terrace. The Duke was at the hub of social and political life and the house played host to the greatest politicians and personalities of the day for three decades.

The Duke suffered heavily in the South Sea Bubble fiasco of 1720 and never made up his losses. When he died in 1744, he left substantial debts and the house and its contents were sold. Too expensive an edifice to be lived in, the great palace was demolished. The site was purchased four years later by a wealthy and successful master cabinet-maker, William Hallett, who erected a smaller but still substantial house in Portland stone. The second owner of the new house was an Irishman, Colonel Denis O'Kelly, best known for his ownership of the famous racehorse, Eclipse. The house passed through several other hands before being placed on the market in the late 1920s by Sir Arthur Du Cros, one-time Lord Mayor of London.

At a meeting on 8 July 1927 Canons, its setting and advantages were described to the Governors. They were won over by the enthusiasm and sound arguments of Miss Drummond and her convert, Dr Brackenbury, and decided unanimously that the School should move. An offer of £17,500 was made and accepted for the house and the grounds which was approved by the Board of Education, after considerable dithering, in December 1928. Middlesex County Council also supported the purchase and made a commitment to covering two-thirds of the purchase price and two-thirds of the costs of adaptation up to a limit of £20,000. The purchase was completed on 9 May 1929 after which four members of staff, Misses

James Brydges, the first Duke of Chandos, who had Canons built in the early 1700s.

The counterpart lease of Canons to a James Hawkins by a John Franklin in 1794.

George Frideric Handel, painted by Thomas Hudson.

The Handel Festival of 1935 – Miss Hayne with nymphs.

Mackreth, Arnold, Pusey and Turpin, were despatched to live in the house where they were to establish a junior school. It was also intended that use should be made of the site for playing fields so the proposed purchase of the Burnt Oak playing field was called off.

Once a week most girls had an opportunity to go up to Canons where, said Miss Drummond, they could enjoy 'fresh air and freedom of movement, the joy of colour, a sense of space and quiet'. One girl remembered that 'The sun shone unremittingly then and playtime was a constant joy. We rushed to climb the Cedar tree and swung from dizzy heights; we basked in the reflected heat down in the empty Roman Bath (on the site of the New School building); we played "hide and seek" in the Rose Garden, raced along the Lime Avenue and even jumped off the wall around Queen's Seat, until we were dazed with fatigue and fresh air.' The pond was used for swimming in summer (girls emerged very muddy if they dived too deeply) and for skating in the winter. The grounds provided the perfect setting for outdoor drama. Another girl recalled that each bright green ticket which took her weekly by train from Finsbury Park to Edgware 'was, in a minor way, a passport to Paradise!'

This was a good start but there were still significant hurdles to be overcome before the whole School could move. Firstly, the London County Council were adamant in their opposition to the move. Here was a school where the number of London pupils had remained constant since before the First World War, where a large number of scholars were being educated at the Council's expense and where the Council had made a substantial investment in the School buildings. Any move would, in the Council's view, disadvantage most London pupils because of the increased travelling time and raise the question of whether the building grant made to the School in earlier years should be repaid. The Council saw no likelihood of being able to take over the buildings to rehouse the Camden School, as was being suggested, and in any case the existing Trust scheme stated that both Schools should be located within the parish of St Pancras.

Some of the LCC's arguments were soon rendered invalid. The Board of Education quickly indicated that it would support a change in the Trust scheme to enable the School to move out of St Pancras. More significantly, the trend for an increasing number of pupils to come from Middlesex at the expense of London pupils continued. Between 1929 and 1934 the proportion of Middlesex pupils rose from 63 per cent to 84 per cent. The number of London pupils fell from 330 in 1926 to 232 in 1935. On the other hand, by far the greater number of scholars in the School came from London (136 to 42).

There remained the question of finance. The economic depression of the early 1930s brought about huge cuts in public expenditure. As a result, stringent curbs were placed on Middlesex County Council's school building programme which made it impossible to contemplate any transfer of North London Collegiate to Canons. The only advantage to the School of this delay was that Middlesex could not proceed with its new girls' secondary school building programme. Schools were being proposed for Mill Hill, Pinner, Wembley and Canons Park (in the event that North London did not relocate) while plans were also afoot to enlarge the Henrietta Barnett School. These plans would make North London Collegiate's location in Camden unviable, given its high proportion of Middlesex pupils.

Another problem was that the LCC, while maintaining its opposition to any relocation of North London Collegiate, was proposing in 1935 after a delay of several years to accede to the request from the Camden School for improved science accommodation with an estimated completion date of 1938. The Governors believed that this would be pointless. The Camden School's buildings were already admitted to be unsuitable. North London's relocation would provide an opportunity for the Camden School to move into the Sandall Road buildings which, although unsuited to North London, would provide Camden with extra space.

All these factors led the Governors to agree in June 1935 that North London should move to Canons by the end of 1938, once the Board of Education had altered the existing Trust scheme. Sandall Road would then become the home for the Camden School whose current site should be sold to the LCC.

The handicrafts room at Sandall Road in 1933.

With the economic recovery permitting a relaxation of restrictions on public spending, a meeting between all the interested parties (both County Councils, the Board of Education, and the Governors) was held in June 1936. The LCC were now more amenable to a move by North London, attracted by the opportunity of acquiring the existing site of the Camden School for further development and of moving the latter to Sandall Road. In these circumstances, Middlesex agreed to delay any plans to complete a secondary school in the Canons Park area until 1939 in order to provide sufficient time for changes to be made to the Trust scheme and for the Camden School to move to Sandall Road. In February 1937 the Governors and the LCC finally came to an agreement over the transfer of North London Collegiate, the sale of the existing site of the Camden School to the Council and the relocation of the Camden School.

The emphasis now switched to planning the School's new accommodation at Canons. In June 1937 the eminent architect, Professor (later Sir) Albert Richardson, was appointed. A significant figure in twentieth century British architecture (one of his later buildings, Bracken House in Cannon Street, built in 1955–59, became the first post-war building to be listed), Richardson was a classical architect with immense respect for the past, qualities which must have seemed ideal given his task at Canons. The Governors had seen an example of his work at Hawnes School near Bedford where an old house had been adapted and extended. They had been impressed 'with the ingenuity with which he had carried out a very difficult task, the architectural beauty of his work, his wide knowledge of materials, and the extraordinarily small cost at which the adaptation had been effected.' The accommodation proposed for Canons included an assembly hall, dining hall, two gymnasia, swimming baths, five laboratories, two art rooms, two craft rooms, a music room, a lecture room, two

The Sports Day 'Lemonade Tea' under the oak tree near the pond, 1938.

libraries and twenty-four classrooms. At the same time the Middlesex County Council agreed to provide a grant of £42,000 towards the costs, with the Governors contributing £20,000.

The problem was that Richardson's plans came in at £95,000. The Governors reluctantly concluded that the difference could not be met. Working closely together, Professor Richardson and Miss Drummond devised new plans. Even these were estimated to cost £77,000 and, on the Board of Education's insistence, had to be pruned back to £70,000 through the omission of six classrooms. The Governors arranged a loan to cover the balance between funds in hand and total expected costs, although Middlesex County Council also agreed to a small increase in their promised grant. In September 1938 the building contract was awarded to Haymills and work commenced. The foundation stone for the new buildings was laid on 5 May 1939. At last everything seemed to be going according to plan. The Second World War put paid to that.

Junior girls pond dipping with Miss Hall, and senior girls sketching, 1949.

4

'An Extraordinarily Good School'

1939–58

And what has the school stood for? Surely the answer is sound learning and scholarship, sturdy independence and freedom to experiment, and above all the spirit of service and a deep sense of membership of a community and of the school as a member of the wider community of the nation's schools.

North London Collegiate School Magazine, 1942–6.

The international situation worsened steadily throughout the summer months. By the end of August matters were so serious that all the girls returned to School on Monday 28 August prepared for evacuation. Each day that week they turned up in anticipation of being sent to some distant part of the country, well away from the bombs which were predicted to rain down upon the capital. A variety of voluntary activities were devised for them while a group of girls assisted Miss Turpin in preparing daily dinners. It was not until Friday 1 September that the order for the evacuation came but Miss Drummond reported to the Governors that 'these days of waiting were most valuable in preparing their spirit and giving an added sense of unity and comradeship.'

The girls, with thirty members of staff, marched in twos from Sandall Road to Kentish Town station. The newspaper placards they passed recorded the coming of war with the headline 'Germans invade Poland' and they heard encouraging cries of 'Cheer up, ducky!' from the local residents watching them go. Embarking on the train, the girls excitedly discussed their possible destinations. Many of them were disappointed when the train only got as far as Luton, with special buses ferrying them from the station to Luton High School.

Half the school, some 240 girls, went to Luton. A handful were sent by their parents to distant parts of the country. But Edgware was outside the evacuation zone and over 200 girls remained at Canons under the supervision of Miss Turpin, Miss Cross and Miss Mackreth. Miss Turpin, the domestic bursar between 1929 and 1962, was a tall and imposing but

Leaving Sandall Road, 1939.

Wardown Park, Luton.
Above: *a lesson on the tiered stone seats around the cricket pitch;* above right: *rounders under a barrage balloon.*

warmly sympathetic woman with an array of chins which quivered on the rare occasions she became angry. Miss Mackreth was warm and caring and took a real personal interest in her charges. For many girls who knew her from this period, she symbolised the School and was regarded with genuine affection.

Among the sea of brown uniforms there were flecks of green from the few girls from the Camden School for Girls who had not been evacuated to Oakham and later to Grantham. At Canons the incomplete new building was put to use. An air-raid shelter was created from the intended cloakrooms where the window spaces were bricked up. Despite a concrete floor and the lack of any apparatus or heating, one of the gyms was allocated for use whenever it proved too wet for games outside. The adjoining changing room was fitted out with trestle tables and spirit lamps and turned into a science classroom. More than eighty volunteers under the guidance of the groundsman, Robbins, dug up part of the grounds to plant potatoes.

It was just as well that the wonderful summer weather lasted well into September for it was three weeks before arrangements had been made for North London girls in Luton to use the High School. Instead, they took their lessons and games in the grounds of Wardown Park, using as makeshift classroom space the tiers of stone seats around the cricket field. At the end of the month they moved into Luton High School, using the premises from 2 p.m. until 6 p.m. every day. Miss Drummond was realistic about the standard of work that could be attained in such circumstances but by the end of term she believed that 'the girls are gaining something from the lack of daily travelling and the absence of the noise and bustle of London life.' The senior girls were bearing up well but their situation, noted the Head Mistress, made them 'quickly moved either to boisterousness or to tears.'

Miss Drummond was irritated that the girls' conspicuous presence in Luton made them easy targets for gossip: 'If a child refuses prunes and custard, or goes out without her hat, or is careless about changing her shoes, the news runs round the town and then comes back to me.' Billeting arrangements were mixed but on the whole proved satisfactory. Anna Braga found herself with a warm, welcoming, kind and friendly couple chosen particularly because they would take in Catholics, an indication of the lingering prejudice which still existed. Charlotte Hajnal-Konji and her sister hated their first billet and were soon moved. Their mother visited them every third Sunday and once brought the girls their favourite German children's books, shocking their hosts. Thelma Woolford, on the other hand, was moved from her first billet to stay with a mean and tight-fisted couple who expected her to share the weekly bathwater at a time when fuel was not short. The strain was not always on the part of the girls. One young mother with a 6-month-old baby on a local council estate had two 17-year-olds billeted with her.

The winter of 1939–40 was as harsh as the preceding summer had been sultry. At Canons, the girls began to feel the cold in the new buildings. The pitches were snow-covered for weeks and the frozen pond provided a rare opportunity for skating. For lessons in the converted changing room, the girls wrapped up warm. Ennis Freedenberg remembered: 'There we sat in our overcoats, gloves and scarves to withstand the cold emanating from the concrete floor and the unplastered brick walls.' At Luton, skating was to be had on the frozen lake in Wardown Park.

The changed circumstances of war were beginning to have an impact on girls and staff. One girl in Luton wrote of her fear as the planes passed overhead, a fear which often lasted through the night before it was dispelled by daybreak. At Canons, staff grew weary from spending their nights fire-watching on the roof of the Old House before taking lessons the next morning. Rationing brought changes to clothing and diet. Uniform gave way to wartime alternatives and the velour and panama hats disappeared in favour of berets with three-coloured cockades. Poor-quality meat

Below left: *the gates to Wardown Park;* below: *skating on the frozen lake.*

Cyclists leaving school, 1940s.

in the dinnertime stews often prompted unfounded speculation among the girls that the war effort had claimed Queenie, the heavy horse who pulled the gang-mower which kept the pitches trim. Because of wartime regulations intended to combat the threat of German spies, the bicycles used by some girls to travel to school had to be kept padlocked to prevent their theft by spies seeking a speedy getaway. The division of the School between Canons and Luton brought the end of the formal Prize Day. The last one took place at the end of 1938 and was replaced by an informal distribution of awards at the final assembly of the summer term. Evacuation and wartime conditions also brought about alterations to the traditional North London school day which eventually settled into the 9.30 a.m. to 3.30 p.m. routine used by most schools.

Pressure from the Governors resulted in permission being given to the School for the new building to be substantially completed during 1940. *The Builder* remarked that 'The new range . . . is entirely different in character from the building which it complements.' Opinion differed as to whether or not this was a virtue. Miss Drummond spoke of 'its spaciousness, its light and air, its simple dignity and beautiful proportions.' But one girl at least felt that the long corridors, deep stair wells and lack of a main entrance made it seem cool and impersonal compared with the atmosphere of the Old House.

The near completion of the building (some rooms remained unfinished) made it possible for the School to be reunited, with the return of the girls from Luton and the final removal of equipment from Sandall Road. The new School buildings were opened on 18 June 1940 and the Bishop of London led a service of blessing on 26 June. At first the girls divided into two camps, the 'Lutonites' and the 'Canonites', but this did not last long. The School roll numbered slightly more than 400 girls. Some parents had not allowed their girls to return to London while others could no longer manage to attend the School because of wartime difficulties, particularly the disruption of transport. The drop in numbers found the School overstaffed and in order to balance the books the staff accepted a temporary reduction in both hours and pay.

As one girl, Pamela Hailey, later wrote, 'things changed. A lot of normal school activities could not be continued, people were expecting personal disasters, raids were becoming heavier and more frequent, so the full reality of war began to come home to us.' The raids inevitably disturbed the pattern of work but the girls continued to study in the shelters.

And there was a change in Head Mistress. Miss Drummond had told the Governors in early 1940 that she intended to retire at Christmas. Unlike her predecessors, she refused to have her portrait painted and none exists but her influence upon the School was indelible. As one writer in the School magazine recorded, 'She was no lover of the "forcing frame" and cared not to produce strange startling growths or "show specimens" but let us grow and develop according to the laws of our being.' That was not to say that academic standards were neglected as the calibre of her staff and the examination records demonstrated. But she redressed the balance between examination-centred study, study for its own sake and a broader range of extracurricular activities. The social and charitable ethos of the School had been underpinned by her promotion of the Frances Mary Buss House and its future secured in often trying circumstances through the move to Canons. The bench she gave to the School which still sits on the South Terrace is inscribed *Hic Amoena Delectent* – 'Here let them enjoy the beauties'. Unsurprisingly, her horizons extended beyond the School. Among other activities, she chaired various committees of the Association of Head Mistresses, toured Canada with other head mistresses in 1931, and was a member of the Consultative Committee of the Board of Education. She was a Governor of the City of London College and the Froebel Institute and a member of the Council of Bedford College. Her services to education brought her the award of the OBE. Modest and self-effacing, her friendliness and sympathy gained her the affectionate nickname of 'Drumsticks'. One girl summed up her generosity of outlook by saying that 'Miss Drummond always thinks that we are so much better than we are.' Mary Darlaston was at the School in the 1920s and nearly seventy years later wrote that the spirit of Miss Drummond was to be found in 'care for one another, sense of belonging, respect for individual needs and ideals, and concern for the outer world.'

Eileen Harold, Head Mistress 1940–43.

Miss Drummond's successor as Head Mistress of the North London Collegiate School had been appointed in July 1940. Of all those considered, Eileen Harold was both the only one not already a head and, at 30, the youngest. Educated at the Hertfordshire and Essex High School in Bishop's Stortford, she had graduated from Lady Margaret Hall, Oxford, with a first-class degree in classics. For three years she had taught at Sherborne School before moving to Haberdashers' Aske's, West Acton, in 1934 in order to be closer to her invalid father. In 1937 she had been appointed second mistress and had taken charge of 200 girls when they were evacuated from West Acton to Dorchester on the outbreak of war. She was highly regarded. The principal of Lady Margaret Hall described her as 'a person of high intellectual capacity, great industry [and] strong purpose' while the head mistress of Sherborne wrote that Miss Harold was 'a delightful girl with a keen sense of humour . . . she would be a popular and stimulating headmistress.' The head mistress of Haberdashers' Aske's was unstinting in her praise of her deputy, recording that she was 'in her generation, the most remarkable person I have ever met.' Eileen Harold, she continued, was a brilliant scholar of wide learning with a deep appreciation of music and art, a teacher with tact and judgement beyond her years and 'a loftiness of thought, aim and life most inspiring to those around her.'

Eileen Harold was a great contrast to her predecessor. Not only was she very young for her appointment, she was also the first Head Mistress of the School to be appointed from outside the staff of the Foundation. While this was an awesome challenge for her, it was perhaps unsettling for many of the long-established members of the staff room. To some girls, she seemed remote and one later confessed that 'I don't think we gave her a very warm welcome.' But remoteness was a characteristic of many head mistresses. Even Miss Drummond could appear distant to those who barely knew her. And Miss Harold was to be found at the end of her first term, standing at the door to the assembly hall, shaking hands and having a personal word with each girl. Other girls delighted in 'her donnish charm, culture, wit and profound faith'. She appears deliberately to have kept a distance between herself, the School and the harsher realities of the world beyond in order to establish at Canons an oasis of peace. She never referred to the 'war', only to 'these difficult times', but the crisis was acknowledged in prayers every week where she drew more criticism for praying for the dead of both sides. She instituted a carol service (the first one took place in 1942) and at one moving Christmas service the girls gave the kiss of peace to the German girls at the School. Perhaps this otherworldliness which she portrayed was at odds with a tradition at the North London Collegiate which, while principled, was practical rather than philosophical.

Her greatest admirers were the more senior girls in the School who appreciated the sharp intellect of this shy, spiritual, self-conscious woman.

For the fifth form upwards, she introduced general studies, opening opportunities for girls to make their first acquaintance with the classical greats such as Plato and Aristotle. For many of them this introduction was a revelation. Her quiet passion for music stimulated a revival in musical standards, as choirs were formed in each year and the redoubtable Mrs Manson was brought out of retirement; and she personally produced the staff play each year, including a notable *St Joan*. Mrs Manson's return to the School was only one example of Miss Harold persuading some of the School's talented retired staff to come back temporarily while younger staff were on war service. Mrs Hatfield, a brilliant teacher of biology who had written a best-selling textbook on the subject, was another instance, having retired only in the summer of 1941.

The return to service of teachers like Mrs Manson and Mrs Hatfield, coupled with the retention of other outstanding staff, enabled the School to maintain examination results which were 'at least as good' as those achieved before the war. Miss Senator, for example, 'fiery tempered, plump and passionate', remained a huge influence on her pupils. Four times a week she took Jewish prayers, bringing order to the chaos which had characterised initial attempts to hold separate prayers for the substantial number of Jewish girls at the School. Miriam Shillito in the English department similarly expected the highest standards from her pupils and demanded that they strove to fulfil their potential. Under staff such as these, education at the North London Collegiate School was characterised during the war by a determination to discover and maximise the strengths of the girls without overlooking their weaknesses. In this the staff were helped by a less intense examination-driven environment. Miss Senator never referred to 'set books' in her sixth-form classes. Her pupils ranged widely over French literature as she sought to teach them more about its development rather than a narrow canon of texts, whose authors she referred to only a fortnight before the examinations.

The war years were strange, restless years for the School yet despite her own inner turmoil Miss Harold represented an influence for steadfastness and stability. Some girls felt themselves largely unaffected by the war and Miss Harold noted to the Governors in the summer of 1941 that 'we do count ourselves most fortunate to be so far free from the real and constantly besetting obstacles with which many schools are daily faced and to find our lot cast in surroundings and conditions which make work a delight.' But there is little doubt that it did have an impact upon many of them, perhaps not through the occurrence of any major event but more because of the way they had to adjust in many small ways.

The frequent air raids of the Blitz saw the introduction of two time-tables, one for use during alerts which enabled senior girls to enjoy some continuity of teaching. Shell fragments hit the cedar tree and brought to an end the enjoyment of climbing it for the younger girls. At Easter 1941

87

Bomb damage in West Hendon, just a few miles south-east of the School, in 1941. It was caused by an experimental bomb which was intended for the air-craft factories further north, but was dropped prematurely. Eighty people died and forty houses were totally destroyed.

Bomb damage inflicted on the Camden School for Girls.

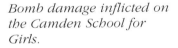

Miss Rigby, who had taught maths at the School since 1923, died as a result of enemy action, bringing to the School a sense of the loss created by war. As a teacher, she was fondly remembered as someone who 'loved to help lame dogs over stiles'. The summer brought the news of the death in action of Sergeant Pilot John Morton, who as a young boy had been taught at the School. Although the air raids continued, they became less severe and they were now taken for granted by the girls who went to their shelters irritated rather than afraid. The reality of war returned to the School in February 1944 when the school captain, Pamela Flowers, was killed during an air raid. Then came the advent of the V bombs during the summer of 1944. Numbers, which had risen to 665 by late 1943, dropped again as many girls were evacuated. More time seemed to be spent in than out of the shelters and during the brief all-clears the girls would wander the grounds collecting pieces of shrapnel and strips of silver anti-radar paper dropped by the flying bombs. Examinations that summer were taken in the cramped, electrically lit shelters where stress and stale air resulted in frequent headaches. Because girls were eligible for call-up on national service at the age of 18 unless they had gained a place at university, Higher School Certificate and university entrance examinations were both taken during the same year which placed additional stress on some senior girls. The V2 rockets which superseded the V1s gave no warning of their arrival so classes just carried on. A rocket landing nearby rattled classroom doors and the aftershock of a distant blast blew back the curtains of the prefects' room. But although some of the experiences were 'alarming and exhausting', the School fared much better than many.

With the shortage of domestic and grounds staff, a rota of girls was drawn up to cover sweeping, dusting, packing, washing and polishing. Much of the burden lay upon Robbins who 'kept all the boilers stoked for us, . . . grew marvellous vegetables and kept the sports ground available for play.' The girls also dug the allotments and knitted garments for the troops. The sixth form organised a concert to raise funds during War Weapons Week. Some girls adopted servicemen. One group of third-formers were allocated a young sailor called Nick Crawford who was 'probably the recipient of more ill-fitting mittens and balaclava helmets than any other sailor in the Fleet'. The girls also created the Nick Crawford Club (membership one penny, newsletter monthly). Membership fees and other contributions brought funds up to £5 so the girls arranged to treat their adopted sailor when he came on leave to London. Twenty of them, chaperoned by a teacher, met him in Piccadilly Circus, showered him with a variety of gifts and took him to the nearby Lyons Corner House for tea. 'We gave him the money that was left over to buy sweets. He probably retired to the nearest pub to recover.'

The girls revived clubs and societies which had been dormant since the beginning of the war and activities were arranged with other schools, including a conference on co-operation for world peace held at Canons during Easter 1943, involving all the secondary schools in Middlesex and North London. Contact was also maintained with the Frances Mary Buss House in Bromley-by-Bow. Senior girls continued to visit the House until the war made this impossible but the girls carried on sending Christmas parcels, clothing and food and raising funds for the House. The Whitsun

Going home, 1949.

89

camps which had been so popular before the war were resumed at Canons under Miss Turpin in 1942. During the Blitz and the V-bomb raids, the House provided shelter for local people, providing many of those bombed out of house and home with food and drink, even though the property itself was very badly damaged at one stage.

The exposure of the girls to experiences which were out of the ordinary and their greater involvement in keeping the School going encouraged their earlier maturity and a strong feeling developed that they should have a greater say in how the School was run. Miss Harold was receptive to the idea and during 1943 the prefects and monitors met with her to discuss the basis for a School Council. There was also an attempt to create a house system and introduce more formal discipline, perhaps reflecting a desire to impose greater order when the outside world appeared to be in such disarray. But 'the North London tradition of personal approach' was reaffirmed. Norma Lee attended the School from 1940 until 1946. Her experience was typical of many both before and since. Discipline was based on the expectation that each girl would behave responsibly. The only rules forbade running in the corridors (since it was dangerous) and excessive noise (since it disturbed others).

Some girls felt that growing up more quickly during the war had deprived them of their youth. Their priorities were different and, while they may have become more mature and independent as a result, their shared experience had brought them almost too close together. This sense of claustrophobia made them yearn to break free of the School and claim their own freedom and privacy. Because of this, few of them kept in touch or joined the Old North Londoners Association after they left.

Towards the end of Miss Harold's headship, the radical Butler Education Act of 1944 was passed. There had been talk prior to the introduction of the Bill that tuition fees would be abolished in Direct Grant schools (that is, those like the North London Collegiate School that were receiving grants from the Board of Education in return for the allocation of free places) as well as in other schools. The arguments rehearsed then against this suggestion would be heard again to less effect thirty years later. The Association of Governing Bodies of Girls' Public Schools opposed the idea on the grounds that it would place governing bodies under the control of local education authorities; that it would deny parents the right to choose; that it would diminish educational standards; and that it would force Direct Grant schools either into independence or into the state sector when they occupied a unique position between the two. The proposal went no further and the School applied to continue as a Direct Grant school when the new regulations appeared in the spring of 1945, an application granted that autumn by what was now called the Ministry of Education.

Eileen Harold was Head Mistress for just under four years, a remarkably brief period of time, even given the fact that her term occurred during the

Second World War. On 27 November 1943 she wrote to the Chairman of Governors, Dr Clay, that 'she had for some time felt doubtful whether she was in the right place at Canons' and that she had been offered the headship at her old school, Haberdashers' Aske's. Dr Clay tried and failed to dissuade her while Miss Gossip, appointed to the new post of second mistress in 1943, wrote on behalf of the staff to the Governors, asking them to try once more to persuade Miss Harold to stay since the feeling of the staff was that 'there was no incompatibility between Miss Harold's ideals and those of the school.' Miss Harold was invited again to reconsider but she reconfirmed her resignation in January 1944. Further light is shed on Miss Harold's departure in a letter written by her predecessor, Miss Drummond, to Miss Harold's successor in September 1944. She wrote that Miss Harold's resignation had come as 'a great shock' to the staff and 'The fact that they had become personally attached to her did not make it easier.' Miss Drummond continued that:

> The life of the school has been largely built up on respect for the individual, effort to understand and meet the needs of the individual and to help her to find her place in the community. We did not more than necessary impose a pattern of behaviour from outside but tried to train the girls to base their behaviour more and more on principle and to see their actions in the light of their effect on other people. To Miss Harold our atmosphere was altogether foreign. She had no confidence in the underlying principles and yet does not seem to have felt that she should transform them.

One Old North Londoner wrote in later years that Miss Harold was a fine and impressive woman but 'we at North London much preferred the more secular, prosaic, down-to-earth Yorkshire woman, Dr Kitty Anderson.'

Born in St Anne's in Lancashire in 1903, Kitty Anderson was brought up in the North Riding of Yorkshire and attended the Saltburn High School for Girls where she became head girl. In 1920 she won a North Riding scholarship to read history at Royal Holloway College, becoming the first pupil from her school to win a university place. She had never been to London before and there was so much excitement at her going that the station platform was crowded with staff, pupils and other well-wishers. It was in history, always one of her great loves, that she secured her doctorate of philosophy in 1933, having returned to the College to study Elizabethan rogues and vagabonds. But she also had a huge interest in the wider world and spent the year immediately after she graduated carrying out social work back in Yorkshire where she also helped with an election campaign in a mining constituency. It was this breadth of outlook, combined with her sharp intellect, which would place her in such harmony with the traditions of the North London Collegiate School. Before studying for her doctorate, she had trained as a teacher at the London Day Training College after which she took up a position in 1926

Katherine Anderson, later to become Dame Kitty, as a student in the 1920s.

Kitty Anderson, 1951.

Kitty Anderson laying the foundation stone of the drawing school in 1957, with her characteristic hat and smile.

at the Craven Street Secondary School, Hull, a maintained co-educational school. As Dr Anderson, she taught at Burlington School in Wood Lane, Hammersmith, becoming second mistress before obtaining her first headship at King's Norton Grammar School for Girls, Birmingham, in 1939. She had barely arrived before she had to arrange the evacuation of part of the school to Gloucestershire. The remainder of the school stayed in Birmingham and Dr Anderson divided her time equally between the two sites, spending a fortnight first in one place and then the other.

The Governors of the North London Collegiate School saw in Dr Anderson's testimonials many of the qualities which made her so suited to the post. As well as her high standard of scholarship, 'she has a most sympathetic understanding of the interests of those pupils who are less successful in the more formal subjects of the curriculum with the result that she has welded the whole school [King's Norton] into a most happy community with both a vigorous and varied life of its own, and a proper sense of its relationship to the outside world.' At Hull she had established excellent working relationships with her colleagues while at the Burlington School her discipline had been based on the friendly and willing co-operation of her pupils.

Kitty Anderson applied for the job in February 1944, writing to her father that she wished as few people as possible to know since she had no wish to unsettle her present school when nothing might come of it. (On the other hand, she knew what she was worth, writing in the same letter that one of His Majesty's Inspectors had told her that 'he regards me as outstanding and that he sees me going on from North London to even greater heights in a space of years but I don't know!') When she heard that she had been placed on the short list for the post, she was so excited that she exhibited one of those very human traits which earned her such affection: 'I went to B[ourne] & H[ollingsworth] and bought a very smart model hat which should give me great courage . . . So even if I do not get the job I have at any rate got a new hat!' Of her appointment, she wrote to her parents that 'it just seems like a dream', attributing her success to them for the sacrifices they had made for her throughout her life.

At her previous school, she was missed for 'her fun and gaiety, her wisdom and her zealousness' but she brought these in abundance to her new school. Never seeming to walk anywhere when she could run, her small frame seemed to contain limitless energy and enthusiasm. She laughed a lot and her warmth and friendliness brought her the adoration of the youngest. With a genuine interest in each girl as an individual, she knew all their names within the first half of her first term. Her relative informality and approachability were a revelation. This was a Head Mistress who would seek out a girl rather than send a summons for her to come to her study.

As a teacher, she inspired many with her vivid teaching style but always encouraged girls to use their initiative to develop their own learning. She

Clement Attlee, with his wife Violet, celebrating the Labour landslide in the 1945 General Election.

would gain a reputation in later years as one of the country's leading educationalists and her advice was much sought after. When she arrived at the North London Collegiate School in the autumn of 1944, she already had shrewd views about the education of girls, views which often had much in common with those expressed by her predecessors. She never forgot the words written to her upon her appointment by Miss Drummond: 'Perhaps the strongest element in our tradition is fearless facing of the future and adaptation of our life to new needs'; and she took them to heart as the School moved from the difficulties of war to the problems of an impoverished peace.

Kitty Anderson believed that 'education is a social service.' In the years of austerity which followed the war when poverty and hardship still accompanied the continued rationing of food, clothing and other materials, Britain was acknowledged to be a drab, dull and often depressing place. Given these circumstances, Dr Anderson had no doubt that education had to take its pupils above and beyond the grind of their daily lives. At the same time, many girls still left school at 15. The pressures upon them to forsake education included the attraction of earning their own living, the financial demands of their own homes, a lack of regard for education from many parents and the continuing prejudice against female education summed up by Kitty Anderson as the attitude of '"Why should she stay at school, she will in any case get married!"' One girl later recalled that 'My parents were not too worried whether I or my sister went on to university as long as my brother did.' So education had to be an attractive proposition in its own right.

Her paper, 'The Education of Girls', prepared in 1951, tackled both these

The School's centenary in 1950. Anticlockwise from top right: *the daffodil procession; 'Foundation Day' tableau vivant; 1950 and 1850 school dress; the opening of the Centenary Gates in 1952.*

points. Aesthetic values had to be nurtured. Taste could not be taught but girls could be given the material for forming it through the quality of their physical surroundings. When many homes had few books, it was important that they were readily available at school and that girls should use them for their own benefit. The ideal curriculum remained the one 'in which all subjects, practical, artistic and academic play a part.' While Kitty Anderson believed that the creative arts were valued in girls' education, she readily admitted that more time might be devoted to them. The stress of focusing too much on public examinations had to be avoided and girls had to be encouraged to learn for themselves. 'The business of learning remains an individual matter,' Dr Anderson later wrote. 'Our aim must surely be to start off our girls on their individual search for truth so that they may, in their own right, experience the joy and wonder of discovery. Equipped they must be for the journey but a surfeit of instruction can smother the desire to explore and sap initiative.' And since most girls, Dr Anderson acknowledged, became wives and mothers, 'school, where they spend such formative years of their life, should not be a place apart from life.' Shared activities with boys' schools, including conferences, dances and club meetings, were important in this regard.

Many of the things she was writing about in 1951 she was already putting into practice at the North London Collegiate. When the war was over, the shelters at Canons were demolished and the cloakrooms completed. Over the next few years the new building was decorated for the first time and the ground-floor corridor was tiled but the School could afford to equip the gyms only partially and had to make use of the benches and cupboards from Sandall Road. The Drummond Library, an improvement on previous library facilities, was opened in 1954.

Efforts were being made to expand the facilities at Canons. In 1943 the parents of Mary Done, who had died while at School, made a gift in her memory to enable an open-air swimming pool to be built. Restrictions

94

both during and after the war caused the scheme to be repeatedly postponed but the pool was opened by the School's patron, the Duchess of Gloucester, on 7 June 1955. Lack of funds also prevented the creation of a badly needed art and craft block. The existing art and craft rooms were scattered throughout the School and could not in any case cope with a School roll which had reached more than 700 by 1951. Two years later, in coronation year, the gardens were landscaped and restocked and a rolling programme of redecoration for the entire School was approved.

More needed to be done but funds would not permit it. To cover the predicted small financial deficit in 1952, the Governors agreed to raise fees to £58 10s. a year for the Upper School and £55 10s. for the Lower School but the Ministry of Education forbade any rise above £54. This meant that revenue spending ate up the additional income and it was impossible to set aside money for capital projects.

Creative activities were encouraged through a system of voluntary periods for each year group when girls could choose from a range of activities. Senior girls, for instance, spent Tuesday afternoons at cookery, pottery, bookbinding, craft, music or dancing.

The first GCE results in 1951 were good but Kitty Anderson deliberately prevented any girl from sitting more than five GCE examinations at O-level. One of these had to be mathematics if the girl was an arts student; the remainder could not include subjects intended to be studied at A-level. Firstly, this dampened the competitive urge to accumulate certificates for the sake of it. Other measures in the same vein included making a girl's grades available only to herself and never in public and the opportunity

The street party to celebrate the coronation of the Queen in 1953 at Fairfoot Road, Bromley, organised by the Frances Mary Buss House, which continued to work with the local population.

A diving display at the opening of the Mary Done swimming pool, 7 June 1955.

95

Creative activities. Above: *Miss Waddington's Form I percussion band in 1955;* above right: *Form III in the craft room with Mrs Cowles, 1949.*

to postpone their external examinations for those who found the pressure too great. Secondly, it was all part of the continuing North London belief in a broad and liberal education for its pupils. One pupil remembered that in addition to her examination subjects she was also able to study current affairs, comparative religion and politics. Many Old North Londoners recall how they were also encouraged to learn for themselves through the provision of private study periods. After the war a sixth daily period for private study had been added after the long lunch break which was still used for extracurricular activities. One girl who left in 1955 later wrote that 'the ethos of being responsible and self-determining in one's approach to

Facing page: *juniors by the pond in the 1990s.*

Right: *Ernest Read's Christmas concert at the Royal Festival Hall, December 1954, in which twenty-seven members of the School Choir took part.*

Main picture: *relaxing in the grounds at Canons*.
Inset: *the sports field*.

work gripped me so that I responded creatively. Here there was time to study on my own in the library: a new way into the discipline of learning. The library became a real joy, and I would happily sit exploring through books after the other girls had gone home.'

One way of encouraging girls to remain at school after the official leaving age was to widen opportunities for sixth-formers. With 120 members in 1945, the sixth form was the largest in the School's history and there was increasing pressure to find a role for the growing numbers of sixth-formers who were not prefects. The School Council, first mooted during Miss Harold's time, came into being during 1945 under the chairmanship of the senior prefect to allow those outside the select band of prefects (who numbered only twenty-four), from the lower-fourth upwards, to feed in their own ideas for improving the running of the School.

There were shared activities with boys' schools. The first annual dance was arranged with sixth-formers from Mill Hill and Aldenham Schools in 1947 and an inter-school discussion group was formed in 1948. Kitty Anderson appreciated the mutual attraction between boys and girls and often welcomed the boyfriends of many of her girls. All this encouraged much more relaxed relationships between the sexes. It was mainly sixth-formers who benefited from the outings and expeditions to museums and theatres which were initiated and the trips abroad which began to occur, the earliest one appearing to have been a classics trip to Italy in 1950. The sixth-form rooms were located in the Old House rather than the new building, creating 'a feeling of home rather than an institution'.

Senior girls reading in the grounds, 1949.

A Frances Mary Buss House trip to Switzerland in 1947.

Close relationships were resumed with the Frances Mary Buss House (weekly fund-raising collections were made in the School) and the Christmas parties for the Aldenham Street School in St Pancras (and later the Edith Neville School) were revived in 1946. But the personal links between the School and the House began to weaken. One girl later remembered that she 'never really got the hang of this exchange'. The girls from the Frances Mary Buss House 'had independence, were out at work, earned money, smoked cigarettes, wore cheap make-up.' Yet the social contrast which North Londoners came across through their own personal involvement also occasionally revealed disquieting facets of their own characters. The same girl recorded how she had been asked to scrub the floor at the House, an experience which she found 'bitterly shaming as I had never done such a thing at home and was not organised or adept at it.'

As some links were weakening, others were being forged in the name of friendship. In October 1949 an exchange visit was arranged between the School and the Goethe Gymnasium für Mädchen in Ludwigsburg, near Stuttgart, and ten girls, with their teacher, Frau Helene Feser, came over to London. Such arrangements were uncommon but by no means unknown among British schools at the time. Latymer Upper School in Hammersmith, for example, had established close links with a German school in Hamburg in 1947, the success of which inspired attempts to forge new relationships with other European schools. It was very much in keeping with the spirit of the post-war age.

At the North London Collegiate School the venture had been inspired by Miss Senator. She had met Frau Jenny Heymann before the war. As a Jew, Frau Heymann was forbidden to teach in state schools and was compelled to leave her post at what was then known as the Goethe Oberschule. At the time she was sharing a flat with her former head mistress, Frau Dr Elisabeth Kranz, who had been forced into early retirement from the Gymnasium because of her liberal views. In 1948, both Elisabeth Kranz and Jenny Heymann, who had escaped from Germany before the war, were reinstated at the school. Caroline Senator returned to Germany to visit her friends and the idea of links between the two schools was born. The relationship has been maintained ever since, giving rise to several long-lasting personal friendships. It also led to a series of links with other schools, initially with the Lycée de Jeunes Filles in Rheims in 1949, then with a number of other French schools and most recently with a school in the United States.

The School's success in meeting the needs and aspirations of pupils and parents may be judged in part from the destinations of its leavers. In 1946 less than 24 per cent of leavers had university places. By 1953 this figure had risen to 35 per cent. This was taking into account the fact that some girls left the School at the end of their first year in the sixth form while many others took only a general arts course rather than A-levels. Below the sixth form, the School was having increasing success in retaining girls for the minimum five years. In 1958, only one girl since 1955 had failed to complete the five-year course. Another indicator of success might be the School's rising roll. By the autumn of 1956, 813 girls attended the School, of whom 188 were in the sixth form, and the buildings were beginning to bulge at the seams. In 1958, there were four applicants for every place with prospective entrants being submitted from sixty-nine primary schools and nineteen independent schools.

Kitty Anderson believed that a university place would open up all sorts of opportunities for her students just as it had for her. But while it was generally accepted that women were entitled to study for degrees (even Cambridge had agreed at last in 1948 to confer degrees upon its female graduates), they still had to fight against continuing prejudice. At the end of the war, for example, the pressure on university places was acute as servicemen returned to complete their interrupted education. In 1946 90 per cent of university places were reserved for them. This was understandable. What was less so was that the bulk of the remaining 10 per cent of places was intended for other male candidates. Under Dr Anderson's leadership, the North London Collegiate School swung into action. Girls wrote directly to their MPs, questions were asked in the House of Commons and ultimately an assurance was obtained that there would be no discrimination in making awards. While it remained very difficult to gain a place, the School did succeed in winning seven open awards. A second example of continuing prejudice concerned medicine. Over the

Upper sixth chemistry with Miss Clark, 1955.

years many Old North Londoners had entered the nursing profession but despite the success of Dr Garrett Anderson so many years before very few women were becoming doctors. One reason for this was that the medical schools restricted female applicants by applying an unofficial quota. Such discrimination only fuelled Kitty Anderson's determination to ensure that as many of her pupils as were able attained admission to university. She changed the minds of many parents who initially saw no good reason why their daughters should attend university and harried admissions tutors into offering places to those girls whose personal circumstances had caused them to perform uncharacteristically badly in examinations. But the pressure for some was too much; one girl recalled 'the tear-stained faces of those who failed [university entrance examinations]'.

Perhaps because of this determination, there was some criticism that the School neglected those who were less academically inclined. Certainly Dr Anderson had no hesitation in admitting that 'We are an academic school. I think that what a young woman needs is the opportunity to develop her mind and to be given as many interests as possible.' Yet the girl referred to earlier who enjoyed the challenge of having time to study by herself confessed to being one of the less academically gifted additions to the School. And Dr Anderson never had any hesitation in issuing a pre-printed circular to the mother of a less able girl, advising that she should drop her weakest subjects and 'pursue a course designed for her capabilities, which would enable her to get the most out of her school course from every point of view, and incidentally would give her a better chance in her public examination,' using the time for extra study in other subjects and in taking up domestic science to examination level.

But domestic science remained, in the opinion of at least one pupil, the most old-fashioned part of the curriculum during the 1950s. For instance, the girls were taught how to scrub wooden tables so they could check whether or not their housemaids were doing it correctly! For all her recognition that most of her pupils would become wives and mothers, Dr Anderson's desire that the School should not become 'a place apart from life' had some way to go.

Dr Anderson recognised the need for those who would not take degrees to receive the training required for a fulfilling career. Between 1946 and 1949, she was a member of the Carr-Saunders Committee on Education for Commerce. She believed it was important that the needs of every pupil should be considered individually so that she might find training which suited her temperament and ability and which offered her 'the joy which comes from the fulfilment of her potentialities.' But even in 1951 she felt that the most appropriate careers for women were in the main limited to 'teaching, nursing, domestic science and institutional management and the branches of social service'. Yet there was an almost unspoken assumption that Old North Londoners should continue pushing back the boundaries

Dr Elizabeth Garrett Anderson, the first woman to qualify as a doctor of medicine in Britain. As a young woman, she was a contemporary of Frances Mary Buss at Queen's College. She received her qualification in 1866.

Relaxing in the staff room, 1949.

for women. The occasional careers talk demonstrated the gap between 'the wonderful breakthroughs for women' which the girls were always being told about and the prosaic realities: 'it never thrilled me that someone had made it in the Geological Survey or as a Factory Inspector.' In any event most girls felt as their Head Mistress did that they would soon be faced with the choice between career and marriage. They simply did not have the role models for women who combined marriage and career.

All this began to change in the late 1950s. After years of enforced austerity, the British economy entered a period of unparalleled prosperity. A booming economy brought virtually full employment and created a million new jobs. Married women provided the only labour available to fill many of these jobs, even in teaching and nursing, for so long the preserve of single women. By 1961, more than half the women in work were married. It did not necessarily follow that since they were in such demand in the market, the market would recognise their worth. In fact, it was teaching, where pay was controlled by the state, which led the way in the introduction of equal pay for men and women. At the North London Collegiate School fees were raised in stages between 1956 and 1961 to accommodate the implementation of equal pay for women teachers.

Dr Anderson was an enthusiastic supporter of married women entering the teaching profession and believed that it should be easier for those who had married and brought up their families to do so. She presided over a staff of high intellectual calibre whose teaching, if not always stimulating, was always diligent. The most outstanding included Kathleen

Gare, a pale, slight woman, gentle but strict and with a strong personal presence: 'she was legendary for being able to quell a dining-hall full of some 300 lively middle-school girls without ever raising her voice.' As a teacher (she was on the staff between 1939 and 1972) her physics lessons were 'a constant source of wonder and delight'. The English mistress, Margery Clay, was 'a woman of genius and a light of inspiration to those she favoured'. As ever at the School, a regular stream of first-rate teachers flowed in and out as they were encouraged to move on to higher things. In 1952, for example, Miss Raeburn was appointed head mistress of Westcliff High School and Miss Marshall was appointed one of Her Majesty's Inspectors.

In May 1958 the School received an official inspection for the first time in twenty-one years. The inspectors' report was a paean of praise for the School and its Head Mistress. The language used in the report was quite extraordinary in the way it applauded the School's performance. Dr Anderson, wrote the inspectors, was 'a distinguished teacher' who had employed 'her stimulating influence' to build up the School which had been enriched by her outside commitments. She 'is never too busy to welcome visitors, to be accessible to every member of the community, and to plan, with vision and practical realism, for the present and future welfare.' 'The work of the school as a whole is very good indeed' and the encouragement given to girls to learn for themselves had produced pupils who 'exhibit independence of mind and judgement to a remarkable degree.'

The School's staff were 'exceptionally able and versatile'. Religious instruction was praised for the 'quality and enthusiasm of its teachers'

Juniors on the terrace in June 1955, some of them playing 'budge', an original North London game which is still played today on what has come to be known as 'budge square'.

102

(Misses Steel, Golden, Clay and Waynforth). The English staff were praised for 'their many individual gifts, their team-work' (Misses Scrimgeour, Clay, Shillito and Waynforth and Mrs Elliot). The history teaching, under Miss Gossip, was of 'consistently high quality'. The geography department possessed 'a well-balanced and very effective team' in Miss Dass, Miss Southgate and Mrs Levy. Miss Senator, the head of modern languages until her retirement that year, was 'an inspiring and stimulating teacher' and Miss Dowding, the head of classics, 'a stimulating and extremely able teacher'. Maths was 'exceptionally well taught' (Misses Dobson, Ayres, Gare, McIntyre, Southgate and Tame) and the sciences employed 'teachers of distinction who display unusual enthusiasm' (Misses Harker, Clark, Gare, Parks, Horder and Mrs Gagarin). The performance of the arts and crafts team, including Misses Angus, Anderson, Keightley and Metcalfe, and Mrs Goodman and Mrs Cowles, was 'above the average'.

Only domestic science and music, which were both recognised as weak spots by girls at the School at the time, were singled out for anything approaching criticism. The library was substandard in its organisation and the facilities for both indoor physical recreation and music were inadequate. This too the Head Mistress already knew. The lack of sufficient resources as always had hamstrung any plans to improve the facilities to a level commensurate with the School's achievements and Dr Anderson in her usual far-sighted way had persuaded the Governors only months before the visit of the inspection team to launch an appeal to raise money for a Buildings and Endowment Fund.

It was, noted the inspectors, 'an extraordinarily good school'. With sentiments which could apply equally well to almost any part of the School's history, they concluded that 'The school is thus meeting in its fourth home the strong tradition of a liberal and scholarly education and at the same time adapting itself successfully to the needs of the age with the vitality and vision which were characteristic of its founder.'

Canons, 1976.

5

'Everyone Matters'

1958–76

The challenge to each one of us is to see to it that our individual contribution to the whole is worthy of ourselves and is the very best that we can give. Let us never forget that 'we are members one of another'.

Founder's Day Address, 1965

As well as the appeal which was launched in 1958, the School benefited from a number of generous donations over the next few years. These included a bequest from Mrs Done, whose family had endowed the fund dedicated towards the outdoor swimming pool, and the creation of a trust for the School by an Old North Londoner, Doris Gregory. A distinguished scientist in her own right, she had married Harry Jephcott who had built up the pharmaceutical firm Glaxo from small beginnings into one of the leading businesses of its kind. Knighted for his services to the industry, he accepted an invitation to become a Governor of the School and his astute financial advice was invaluable to the North London Collegiate for more than two decades. The trust established by his wife was based on the gift of 5,000 ordinary shares in the company.

During the next few years the School embarked on its first capital projects, apart from the swimming pool, since the completion of the 'new building'. The new drawing school, also designed by Sir Albert Richardson, was completed in 1958 and officially opened by the Duchess of Gloucester on 19 February 1959. The old art room became a music room, although music facilities remained less than satisfactory, and a new physics laboratory was added. Growing sixth-form numbers, which soon exceeded 200, meant that a room intended for storage had to be converted as a classroom.

Kitty Anderson's external commitments grew. In 1959 she was appointed a member of the University Grants Committee and was part of the UK Delegation to the Commonwealth Education Conference held that year in Oxford. In 1960 she was appointed to the Robbins Committee

Above: *the new drawing school, and,* below, *the Duchess of Gloucester with Dr Anderson at its opening in 1959.*

whose brief was to review full-time higher education and which recommended in 1963 its expansion and the creation of new universities. As a member of the Committee, Dr Anderson argued in favour of greater opportunities in higher education for married women from which their early marriages and responsibilities in bringing up their families would otherwise have deprived them and the Robbins Report included several recommendations to this end. For her services to education, she became Dame Kitty in the 1961 New Year's Honours List. She indicated in the summer of 1964 that she wished to retire as Head Mistress at the end of August 1965 and further external appointments came her way during her last year at the North London Collegiate, including membership of the National Council for Academic Awards and the chairmanship of the Council of the Girls' Public Day School Trust.

In her final year, the School was the subject of a BBC documentary which took its title from one of Dame Kitty's addresses – 'Everyone Matters'. After it was transmitted on 3 June 1965, Dame Kitty was deluged with letters from viewers, nearly all of them complimentary, and she replied personally to each one. The programme, without commentary, displayed the warmth and lively informality of the School through its Head Mistress, her staff and pupils. Viewing the film today, one is struck by Dame Kitty's relaxed attitude and deft touch. In her simple and comfortable clothes, her hair tied back into her characteristic small bun, talking in her softly spoken, almost genteel, Yorkshire accent, she comes across as a favourite aunt, shrewd, sympathetic and smiling. One small incident during the film reveals her presence of mind, powers of concentration and concern in the smallest detail for others. Midway through her Founder's Day address, a member of the platform party on her left begins to cough. Without pausing, turning aside or interrupting her prepared speech, Dame Kitty organises a glass of water to be poured from the jug on her right which she silently and skilfully passes to the suffering guest.

Many of the girls in the film show the independence of mind which had seemed such a distinct characteristic of the School to Her Majesty's Inspectors in 1958. They are vivacious, direct and confident, influenced not only by the example of their Head Mistress, whose own teaching style is infectious, but also by the rest of the School's staff. Pupil participation in class appears to be the rule rather than the exception. Girls engage in free and open debate with each other during a civics lesson under Dame Kitty, while in another class a young Asian girl explains Hinduism to her classmates. One television critic wrote that the girls 'worked and argued and sang and sewed and laughed and ate with a tremendous zest which made one feel that the future is going to be better than anyone dared to hope.'

Dame Kitty saying goodbye to each member of the School on her last day.

Dame Kitty with junior monitors on Founder's Day, 1961.

Madeline McLauchlan: behind her is the bust of Frances Mary Buss.

One Old North Londoner from this period, Esther Rantzen, remembers with gratitude Dame Kitty's lessons about democracy, the importance of voting, safeguards against propaganda, and the right of people of all cultures to respect for their beliefs and an honourable place in society; she also much appreciated (as a 'not very conscientious' pupil) being encouraged to develop her non-academic talents in, for example, putting on pantomimes and revues.

By the time of Dame Kitty's retirement, more than half of all leavers were entering university. In 1964, sixty-three leavers out of 123 had university places. Of the remainder, forty-two were going on to the further training Dame Kitty deemed to be so important, ranging from secretarial college and sandwich courses to technical college and teacher training. For Dame Kitty, this demonstrated the success not only of the North London Collegiate School but also of the Direct Grant system. She believed that the system safeguarded choice in education and enabled talented young people to benefit from a good education regardless of their social circumstances. In 'Everyone Matters', she points out that most of the girls admitted every year to the North London Collegiate School came from local primary schools. She also points out that as well as the free places guaranteed under the Direct Grant system, the Department of Education also subsidised school fees and operated a scheme which remitted fees according to parental income. The extent to which the Direct Grant influenced the character of the School may be judged from the fact that in 1964–65 414 of the 754 pupils in the Upper School were holders of free places.

But even before she left the School, the future of a system which the North London Collegiate had been part of since 1926 was starting to be questioned. The Inner London Education Authority, resulting from the reorganisation of local government in London, appeared likely to reduce the number of free places which its predecessor authorities had always taken. The battle over the future of the Direct Grant would last a decade and take up much of the time and energy of the School's new Head Mistress.

Madeline McLauchlan was already head mistress of the Henrietta Barnett School when she was appointed to the North London Collegiate School in December 1964. Her own life and career had brought her into contact with many of the threads which made up the North London Collegiate tradition. She had been educated at the King Edward VI Grammar School for Girls in Birmingham, not far from where Dame Kitty had obtained her first headship. Like Dame Kitty, she had studied at the Royal Holloway College, although her subject was French. After teaching at Shrewsbury High School she found a post at Manchester High School for Girls, where Sara Burstall had been so influential, in 1952. Two years later, a travelling scholarship with the English Speaking Union took her to the United States. Soon after her return she was appointed deputy head at Manchester High and in 1958 she became head mistress of the Henrietta Barnett School where Sophie Bryant had given her advice so freely at the beginning of the century.

Madeline McLauchlan came away from Henrietta Barnett with praise from all concerned. She had taken over the school a year after the death of the previous head mistress. The School was in the middle of unresolved negotiations regarding its Voluntary Aided status and was unable to overcome the inadequacy of its existing buildings by moving to a proposed new site because of the imminent reorganisation of London's local government. Despite all this, wrote the Education Officer for the Borough of Hendon, Miss McLauchlan had imbued the school with a new spirit and had influenced everyone by 'her charming personality, courteous manner and width of outlook'. One of her former parents related how 'by her own ethical standards and her personality, she has directly inspired a good and improving standard of discipline, self-respect and behaviour among the girls at a time when so many influences might have worked the other way.' Her Chairman of Governors pointed to her excellent teaching, the strength of her relationship with pupils, staff, parents and Governors, her expansion of the sixth form and her aptitude for appointing first-rate staff.

An elegant, well-dressed woman, she had a sense of fun and was an easy communicator. She loved conversation and enjoyed telling the occasional tale. She also loved parties, either as hostess or guest. She was not in the mould of the remote and aloof head mistresses of old. Her staff would find that she had a strong belief in working together, finding time for discussions with them whether at the weekly staff meeting or over coffee or at lunch, and in encouraging initiative. Supportive and sensitive to the needs of others, she was the first person one could turn to in a crisis.

At her first assembly in her new school on 16 September 1965, Madeline McLauchlan told the girls that 'this school will only go on being wonderful if we live wonderful lives in it and outside it. Much is required of us to whom so much is given.' A month later, the Department of Education issued circular 10/65, instructing all local education authorities to submit plans for comprehensive reorganisation and it seemed as if the School as it was then constituted might not go on very much longer at all. The reality of the threat was brought home by the Public Schools Commission established in 1966, part of whose remit was to consider how best the Direct Grant schools might be brought within comprehensive reorganisation and whether the central government grant should continue. Dame Kitty Anderson was the only Head Mistress appointed to the Commission and she found it a deeply frustrating and unsatisfactory experience. With two colleagues, T. E. P. Howarth and John Davies, she signed a note of dissent when the Newsom Report, as it was called after the chairman of the Commission, was published in February 1968. The dissenters concluded that 'we believe that the majority of our colleagues are in danger of trying to achieve the best at the cost of the good. We believe that our more modest proposals . . . could set affairs in motion in such a way that this problem will eventually cease to engender the sterile and excessively doctrinaire controversy by which it is at present bedevilled.' Their hopes were to be confounded.

At the North London Collegiate School, the Governors discussed circular 10/65 in depth during late 1965 and early 1966. In July 1966 Miss McLauchlan wrote to the Director of Education in the Borough of Harrow with the School's response. The Governors would be happy to meet their obligations under the circular by admitting more girls into the sixth form but not at the expense of creating too large a school and so destroying the vital personal quality of the School's work. The School wished to continue as an 11–18 school, serving a wide area in order to maintain the wide-ranging social background of its entrants, and to carry on exercising some selection. The School remained as popular as ever. There had been 287 candidates for 105 places in 1966 and the School had admitted forty-nine free place holders and fifty-six fee-paying entrants based on an assessment of which girls could most benefit from attending the School.

As part of the Frances Mary Buss Foundation, the Camden School for Girls was also undergoing a period of uncertainty. In 1966 the ILEA proposed to amalgamate the school with another near by to form a much larger girls' comprehensive school. Since the Camden School was much more a part of the state system, its transformation into a comprehensive was not in doubt. But the Governors, a number of whom were also Governors of the North London Collegiate School, were determined that as far as possible any such transformation should respect the traditions of the Foundation. It was a long, hard and difficult fight but the result was that ten years later the Camden School for Girls remained in existence as a comprehensive school for 750 girls, with additional buildings to accommodate them and sixth-form facilities provided through a consortium of other local schools.

In 1970 the ILEA ceased taking up free places at the North London Collegiate School. It was rumoured that the second report due from the Public Schools Commission advocated the abolition of fees in Direct Grant schools. The Governors decided that in such circumstances they would retain control of the School in order to preserve its character and high standards. This was in spite of the fact that the composition of the Governors had recently been altered to provide the ILEA with five places. A key influence alongside Miss McLauchlan was the then Chairman of the Governors, Dr Edward Carpenter, for many years the Dean of Westminster. He was a persuasive and forceful voice for the retention of the School's independence, winning over dissenters.

The second report of the Public Schools Commission was published in May 1970. Only days before, Miss McLauchlan had addressed the School at Founder's Day. On the Direct Grant system, she told her audience that 'this subtle blending of freedom and control (for we are answerable to the Department of Education and to the community we serve in the use of our resources) would have warmed Miss Buss's heart. She shared our contention that no girl should be denied, for financial reasons, an education fitting her gifts.' But Miss McLauchlan was clear about the route which the School should take in the event that circumstances altered. Bearing in mind that 71 per cent of sixth-form leavers that year had won university places, she continued that 'This is an age in which we need the talents of every highly educated woman. Her worth cannot be overestimated and we must never, by superficial thinking and acceptance of doctrinaire ideas which we have not fully examined, commit ourselves to a course where our present contribution to higher education in a variety of fields would be less effective.'

The report of the Public Schools Commission recommended the end of the Direct Grant. The North London Collegiate School would be one of 177 schools affected. Miss McLauchlan felt that such a step 'will only make the division between the independent sector and the state sector bigger than it has been for years.' She believed as a result that the School would become 'a school for the well-to-do' as full independence from the state inevitably raised fees.

Life continued as normal at the School despite all the political uncertainty. While the Governors had to bear in mind the financial consequences of possible independence, they saw no reason for this to postpone improvements to the fabric of the School. A second appeal was launched to raise funds for a phased development plan. Drawn up in 1968, this encompassed a variety of projects from a sixth-form common room and an all-weather hockey pitch to a music school and more science laboratories. The appeal was augmented by a generous gift from Sir Harry

The opening of the music school, 1973.
Above: *the Duchess of Gloucester enters the building;* below left: *the orchestra performs for the guests;* below right: *the Duchess is waved farewell by the girls.*

Dido and Aeneas *produced in 1966. Dido and Belinda* (top*) and the programme.*

and Lady Jephcott. Initially, it was possible to fund only the common room (which took the name of the Anderson Room), the music school and the science laboratories. The laboratories, named after Sir Harry Jephcott, were opened by Lady Jephcott on Founder's Day in 1972 and the music school by the Duchess of Gloucester on 10 May 1973.

Music was one of Miss McLauchlan's great loves and she did much to encourage its development. Malcolm Williamson, later Master of the Queen's Music, was a notable speaker to the Music Society in 1966 and the School performed *Dido and Aeneas* once more in the same year. The music staff, under Miss Godden, was strengthened by new appointments made by Miss McLauchlan such as Margaret Semple who came to the School in 1969. She was an outstanding musician, with gold medals in piano and organ from the Royal Conservatory of Toronto. She revitalised the teaching of music, established the School's excellent reputation for chamber music and directed many of the musical dramas produced at the School. Senior concerts became more adventurous. In 1972, the concert included a performance of *Three Pieces for Orchestra* composed by the president of the Music Society, Judith Weir, who subsequently became one of the leading composers of her generation. The development of music in the School was helped further when Lady Jephcott endowed an annual scholarship for a gifted musician in 1974. The Jephcotts gave generously to the School yet refused to accept public credit for their kindness. But on Sir Harry's death in 1978 the School choir sang at his memorial service at

The art exhibition for Founder's Day, 1961.

St Margaret's, Westminster, where the Dean, Dr Carpenter, gave the address and which Miss McLauchlan organised.

The School had a strong reputation in art. An Old North Londoner, Peggy Angus, was head of art between 1947 and 1970, instigating the tradition at the School that art should be taught by practitioners. She herself became well known as a tile and wallpaper designer and many of her pupils became distinguished artists, architects and designers. 'Historical reference was the basis of Peggy's teaching, not in a dry, remote or wordy way, but by looking at works themselves or reproductions or reconstructions of them, and making personal works based on them.' Her successor as head of the department, Moy Keightley, had been recruited by Peggy Angus herself in the 1950s. Her paintings are found in collections all over the world and a number of her students achieved eminence in painting, print-making and design. Her successor as head of art, Robina Barson, later recalled that Moy Keightley 'brought her own vision, humanity and humour – her repertoire of magic – to the job and found that she had a capacity of engaging the imagination through her unexpected, vivid way of presenting ideas.' Many girls found the art department, with its staff of strong and talented individuals, a place of sanctuary in the School. They often subsequently found that the calibre of staff at the School outshone that at an art school. Miss McLauchlan's skill for making good staff appointments ensured that this reputation continued under those who joined the department in the early 1960s.

The mural unveiled in 1965.

113

One of the main changes, as far as the rest of the curriculum was concerned, was the end in the early 1970s of restricting girls at O-level to sitting examinations in subjects they would not continue to A-level. This was because of increasing pressure from the universities for a direct link between the two examinations. But science, which many girls had shunned, saw a remarkable revival thanks to improved communications between the separate departments involved and within a year or so more than half the girls in the School were making the sciences one of their options. Science at the School also benefited from Miss McLauchlan's appointment as a Governor of Imperial College, London.

The School maintained its long-standing reputation for attracting fine speakers to meetings of its many societies. Between 1966 and 1970, for example, the Current Affairs Society heard from the General Secretary of the TUC, George Woodcock; Veronica Wedgwood on the art of historical research; Cyril Smith on communism; Dr Ian Byatt of the LSE; the South African journalist, Ruth First; Jo Grimond, leader of the Liberal Party; and from eminent Conservative Iain MacLeod. Drama included a joint production of *Romeo and Juliet* in 1967 with the boys of Haberdashers' Aske's School which was then taken on tour to Germany. Sporting choice now encompassed fencing, table tennis, badminton, judo, volleyball and trampolining while the first organised skiing trip took place during the Christmas holidays in 1974 with a visit to the Bernese Oberland.

A display of English folk dancing at the Bromley Open Day in 1966.

Canons Market, July 1972.
Above left: *football;* above:
the market stalls.

Links remained with the Frances Mary Buss House but the House had outlived its usefulness. New housing developments in the area were accompanied by the provision of social amenities for all ages. When a new comprehensive school was opened locally in September 1968 with its own youth wing, it was decided to close the House. The property was let first to the Federation of Boys' Youth Clubs and then in the late 1980s to the local branch of the charity MIND which eventually rebuilt the House as a drop-in centre with an outreach programme for the mentally ill.

By the time that the House closed, the School was already involved with other forms of community service, including Shelter, assisting the physically disabled and mentally ill, teaching immigrant children, working in hospitals and visiting the elderly. Much of this work was done in association with other schools. In 1969 the name 'Canonaid' was coined to cover all these activities.

In one way or another this all sought to build on the School's tradition for a wider outlook. The girls heard opposing points of view from different speakers as well as expert opinion on topics of broad interest. Social work, excursions, trips abroad, all these took them beyond the boundaries of the School into the outside world. At Founder's Day in 1968 their Head Mistress also reminded them that while much had been achieved for their sex there was still a lot to do: 'Now women are free for the most part to order their own lives and can take their places in almost any sphere of usefulness. But there are still too few places for girls in our medical schools, only twenty-five women sit in the House of Commons, and we had to wait until 1967 until women were appointed Presidents of the Oxford and Cambridge Unions, and till 1968 for our first woman airline pilot. The priesthood of the Church and the Stock Exchange are still

The herbaceous borders.

closed to them. Much still remains to be done – which means for you to do.' Miss McLauchlan herself was particularly active in her fight to break down the barriers still met by girls applying to study medicine. The editorial in the 1970 issue of the School magazine reminded its readers that medical schools still imposed quotas on the numbers of women they admitted, that only now were some male colleges at Cambridge opening their doors to women, that in 1969 average earnings for women in all occupations were still 50 per cent lower than for men. In spite of all this, of course, the real world could still come as a shock to leavers. Encouraged to believe that they could achieve anything based on ability and merit, many of them discovered that in fact women were still seen 'as very different: there were things they were not allowed to do.' The world presented them with 'its chauvinism and . . . barriers that the driving, positive ethos of the school had simply discounted.'

Then there were those girls who believed that what they saw as the academic ethos of the School worked against the interests of those perceived to be less than academic, dashing their hopes and their confidence. One Old North Londoner recalled that the School was 'terrific for academics and girls with a lot of confidence but not so much fun for others' while another felt that in her last two years 'she had been written off academically and that no attempt was made to assess individual skills or to encourage the development of non-academic talents and abilities.' Several Old North Londoners related how they had gone on to achieve qualifications and careers which staff at the School had considered to be quite beyond them.

Perhaps the problem was that in some quarters old habits died hard. It was certainly an issue of which the Head Mistress and her successors were aware and which they sought to alter but changing long-standing attitudes took time. One way in which Miss McLauchlan tackled the problem was to ensure that as much recognition was given to girls who pursued practical or vocational careers as was given to those who followed an academic path. This recalled not only the time of Miss Drummond but also that of Frances Mary Buss herself.

Yet even those girls who felt that they had been neglected at the School recognised the outstanding quality of the teaching which the School offered. One Old North Londoner believed that the teaching she received was more rigorous than that she subsequently experienced at either Cambridge or Stanford. Many distinguished and long-serving members of staff retired during this period, including Miss Shillito, Miss Scrimgeour, Miss Manson, Miss Steel, Miss Clay, Miss Gare, Miss Lewis, Miss Dobson, Miss Angus and Dr Apt, all outstanding practitioners in their respective fields. Kay Steel, for example, taught religious education for nearly twenty years. She was 'witty and warm and an inspirational teacher . . . the privileged group taking Advanced level Scripture could, within forty minutes,

116

touch on Tolstoy, the Suffragettes, Bach, Keats, Victor Gollancz, Paul Nash and Francis Thompson before continuing with the Book of Job!' Alice Apt was head of German from 1959 until 1975. A German Jewish refugee from the Nazis, she inspired countless pupils to enjoy learning German, often filling them with her own passion for German literature. These retirements virtually marked the end of an era. When Miss McLauchlan was appointed Head Mistress, she led a staff where the twenty-nine members with more than ten years' service were all unmarried. This had been the pattern ever since the days of Miss Buss. By the mid-1970s married members of staff were becoming much more common and, thanks to the shrewd judgement of successive Head Mistresses, their talent, ability and commitment matched that of those remarkable women who must once have seemed irreplaceable. Among their number were Mrs Pamela Parsonson who came to the School as head of maths in 1974 and eventually went on to become head mistress of the Francis Holland School, Clarence Gate, in 1987, and Mrs Naomi Rutstein who taught Jewish religious studies at the School from 1969 and built up close ties with many through the warmth and exuberance of her personality. Some of the new members of staff were even men, such as Martin Harrap, appointed head of science in 1976 and an outstanding teacher of physics.

The election of a Conservative Government in 1970 did nothing to remove the uncertainty surrounding the future of the Direct Grant, the abolition of which remained part of the Labour Party manifesto. When the Governors considered independence in 1972, they discussed the possibility of ensuring that the School roll was sufficiently large to enable fees to be set at a level which could provide continuing assistance to a quarter of the annual intake. With this in mind, they felt that it would be necessary to enlarge the 7-year-old intake and establish a junior school. They also recognised that independence would mean reconstituting the Governing Body, providing an opportunity to add business, financial and

Juniors in an art class (below left) *and in the dining room* (below).

117

The Old North Londoners'
Centenary Dinner in the
Clothworkers' Hall, 1973.

educational expertise to their ranks. In the following year the Borough of Harrow followed the ILEA's example and no longer took up free places at the School. To maintain the School's eligibility for Direct Grant status and in keeping with the School's fundamental philosophy of minimising financial barriers to entrance, the Governors decided to provide ten free places themselves. The Governors also accepted the generous offer made by the staff to finance one free place for a year.

The Labour Party returned to power in 1974. Despite its wafer-thin majority, the new Government pressed ahead with its commitment to abolish the Direct Grant. In March 1975 the Secretary of State made his announcement that the Grant would be phased out. The Direct Grant schools immediately launched a public campaign to oppose this move. The North London Collegiate School was one of twenty-nine Direct Grant schools from London and the South-East which joined together locally and Miss McLauchlan, who was a member of the Direct Grant Committee of the Independent Schools Joint Council, took a leading role in the campaign. She received many letters of support although there was one notable letter to the contrary. This came from several Old North Londoners who had been at the School in the 1960s. They argued that the School was retreating from its traditional position in the vanguard of educational progress by refusing to contemplate comprehensive reorgan-

118

isation, which they regarded as the fairest way of encouraging all children. A note clipped to the letter in preparation for a response lists the counter-arguments: accepting that comprehensive education was an ideal which could not be quarrelled with, it was nevertheless senseless to abolish the Direct Grant when independent schools still existed; in pursuing this policy, the Government was creating social division based on wealth; and many parents were desperate to pay for a better education for their children rather than send them 'to the shambles that are London comprehensives'.

The Governors met on 3 July 1975 to decide their response to the statement from the Secretary of State that the Direct Grant would cease with effect from 1 August 1976. The choice lay between joining the state comprehensive system or the ranks of the independent schools. By nine votes to four, the Governors opted for independence. The Governors and Miss McLauchlan believed that it was essential to raise funds for bursaries to protect the character of the School which had been influenced since 1904 by the admission of talented girls from less affluent backgrounds. The phasing out of the Grant meant that the last of those holding free places would leave in the early 1980s. There was never any likelihood that the shortfall in places left by the end of the Direct Grant would not be made up by fee-paying entrants. But this inevitably had an effect on the social composition of the School, particularly since most primary schools, which had once been the main providers of applicants, no longer encouraged their parents to consider the possibility of sending their daughters to the North London Collegiate School.

An external fund-raiser was appointed for six months and the secretary of the Parents' Guild, Mrs Coysh, acted as unpaid appeal secretary. Each day she prepared a list of those who had contributed to the appeal and each day Miss McLauchlan would compose a hand-written note of thanks to every contributor. In aid of the appeal the Head Mistress spoke at forty-four meetings of Old North Londoners arranged all over the country, from Edinburgh to Exeter, Liverpool to Brighton. Indeed, the involvement of the Old North Londoners' Association was a key factor in the success of the appeal. Many members of the School's staff contributed towards the appeal, paying as much as they could afford. Recent leavers sent in money earned from their holiday jobs. The Governors had been advised that they would be fortunate to raise a quarter of a million pounds from the exercise. Within eighteen months a million pounds had been raised.

The appeal also generated a huge amount of goodwill. Within the School it led to the creation of what has since become a North London tradition, the 'Canons Follies'. The first production of this annual variety show took place on 29 March 1976. The sixth-formers who came up with the idea had three aims: to produce an all-female show; to lighten up the School's image; and to contribute towards the appeal fund. It provided an

A Chinese dragon at the summer fête, 1976.

opportunity for girls to display talents which would not otherwise have found an outlet and it involved more than 200 participants from the upper third to the upper sixth as well as staff. It was a great success, watched by an audience of 600, and raised £200 for the appeal.

But it was realised that the School would never raise enough money to replace the free places made available under the Direct Grant system. For that to have happened, the School would have needed to find three million pounds. So at the same time Miss McLauchlan and her colleagues at other schools began to devise a possible alternative. The result was the Assisted Places Scheme which was unveiled to an invited audience of 500 guests at the North London Collegiate School and became part of the Conservative Party's manifesto. It was introduced by the Conservative Government in 1981 and, while it never made up the deficit left by the abolition of the Direct Grant, it helped to reduce it in combination with the bursaries being provided by the School.

Sketching by the pond.

The McLauchlan Library,
opened in 1999.
Inset: *the 'Octagon'.*

*Sesquicentenary
Service of
Commemoration,
St Paul's Cathedral,
5 May 2000.*

6

'Everybody Has Talents'

1976 ONWARDS

The most important characteristics of the school go on applying throughout the generations – the importance of giving opportunities to girls to develop their gifts – whatever they are – with the assumption that they can do anything for which they are willing to work.

An Interview with Miss McLauchlan in the
North London Collegiate School Magazine, 1985.

The ethos of NLCS probably hasn't changed since Frances Mary Buss. It has just evolved with the times, keeping true to its original aims.

Old North Londoner in *ONLine*, No. 2 Autumn 1996.

Independence did nothing to impair the School's academic standards. In 1978 a record twenty-six North Londoners won places at Oxbridge. In 1982 the A-level pass rate was 94 per cent with 64 per cent at grades A and B. By now 80 per cent of leavers in the upper sixth form went on to higher education. As many as a quarter were being accepted to study medicine while very few entered nursing. Others chose to study subjects previously largely the preserve of men, such as physics, astronomy, computer studies, engineering and law. Miss McLauchlan's sterling efforts to encourage greater interest in the sciences had paid off. In fact, the North London Collegiate School was exceptional among girls' schools in having more girls studying the sciences than the arts at A-level. At the same time more girls were applying to art colleges, showing that there was also a wider appreciation of non-scholastic careers. The School remained popular with prospective parents and there were few difficulties in attracting applicants. The bursary appeal and the Assisted Places Scheme ensured that 'no girl had been deprived of a place in the School for want of financial assistance with fees.' By 1983, ninety-six girls were benefiting from bursaries awarded by the School and another thirty-nine were receiving assistance under the Assisted Places Scheme.

HMS Pinafore, *produced in 1982. Miss McLauchlan is in the choir, on the far left of the picture.*

Taking the draw: a lacrosse lesson in the early 1980s, when the game was becoming the school's main winter field sport.

A presentation at the 1982 Sports Day.

But Miss McLauchlan lamented 'the increased emphasis that there is on examination results'. She felt strongly that 'The most important thing is the development of personality and character, together with the development of gifts.' This was reflected in the broad cultural atmosphere within the School. During the late 1970s and early 1980s girls were privileged to hear such speakers as Nicky Henson, Ian Ogilvy, Tom Conti, Reginald Bosanquet, Sian Philips and Peter O'Toole. For the Current Affairs Society in 1984, Ken Livingstone spoke without notes to a packed audience for three-quarters of an hour. He suggested at the end of his talk that the Society should invite someone of the opposite political persuasion and as a result Shirley Porter accepted an invitation to speak. One of the musical highlights of this period was the celebration of the tercentenary of the birth of Handel, who had been closely associated with Canons, with a programme of his music performed by the girls under the director of music, Miss Godden, on the terrace during the summer of 1985. The sporting activities on offer were increasing year by year. By now they covered volleyball, hockey, lacrosse, netball, badminton, tennis, rounders, athletics and swimming. One change was the gradual move from hockey to lacrosse as the main field sport in winter. But a sign of the times was indignantly noted in the School magazine's sports report in 1981: 'Increasingly, our school teams are not returning home unbeaten. Some girls no longer find that being members of school teams is important to them. Music lessons, part-time jobs and weekends away from home are all attractive alternatives to Saturday morning matches.'

But independence and the need to provide bursaries did mean that the School's finances had to be kept under constant scrutiny by the Bursar, Lieutenant-Commander Corby, and his successor, Mr Duly. Facilities could not have been improved without a number of generous bequests. One such bequest came from a late Old North Londoner, Dr Frances Hamer, whose distinguished scientific career had been spent working on the development of colour photography. This enabled the conversion of the former lecture room into a new chemistry laboratory, the John and Mary Hamer Laboratory, and the construction of the 'Octagon', which provided a new lecture room and a workshop theatre. A further bequest of similar size came from the estate of Dr Kenneth Harries of University College Hospital whose wife had been a pupil at the School. The complex was named the McLauchlan Theatre and both the theatre and the laboratory were officially opened by the Duchess of Gloucester on 17 May 1983.

Madeline McLauchlan retired as Head Mistress in December 1985. As her predecessors, so she too had not confined her energies to the North London Collegiate School. She had been a member of the Universities Central Council on Admissions since 1968. She chaired the Scholarship Committee of the English Speaking Union and was vice-chairman of the National Youth Orchestra. She served for twelve years on the executive of the Association of Head Mistresses, including a term as chairman, until it amalgamated in 1978 with the Headmasters' Association, serving on the council of the amalgamated body for a further three years. On her

The Duchess of Gloucester and Madeline McLauchlan at the opening of the McLauchlan Theatre in 1983.

Kay Moore teaching in the McLauchlan Theatre.

123

Joan Clanchy, Head Mistress 1986–97, taking a class.

retirement, the Chairman of Governors, the Honourable Mrs Lindy Price, wrote that 'Madeline McLauchlan's own attitudes and sensitivity have ensured that our standards have not declined and that North London has achieved, as its founder would have expected, an admirable combination of modernity and optimism.'

Joan Clanchy had the distinction of being the only applicant for the post to be short-listed for interview. The Governors considered her to be the outstanding candidate. She was also the first married woman to become Head Mistress. Born as Joan Milne, she was educated at St Leonard's in Fife where she became head girl. She studied modern history at St Hilda's, Oxford, where she was senior scholar. Shortly after leaving Oxford, she married Michael Clanchy. After teaching at Woodberry Down comprehensive school in London, she was appointed as head of history at Park School in Glasgow. Her husband became reader in medieval history at Glasgow University. In 1976 she became head mistress of St George's School for Girls in Edinburgh.

In the words of one of her colleagues at North London, Joan Clanchy was 'absolutely dynamic', bursting with energy, teeming with new ideas. She was fond of describing herself as 'the last of the Catherine the Great school of management', an acknowledgement that she could be poor at delegating. But she tempered this through creating excellent relations with members of staff, for whom her door was always open (as indeed it was for pupils). While she had very decided opinions of her own, she was also very receptive to ideas from others. She came to know the girls by

Playing 'Budge' around the statue of Cupid.

The dining room in 1986.

continuing to teach and got on very well with their parents. She was a witty speechmaker and devised captivating assemblies.

Coming from St George's, she was impressed by the extrovert and open nature of the girls and the School's friendly and informal atmosphere. But a number of changes were made almost immediately for the more effective running of the School. These included shorter assemblies to create a longer break; the abolition of the custom of preparing classroom exhibitions on Founder's Day; and the introduction of a new canteen system which provided healthier food and was less costly to run.

Another issue reviewed by Mrs Clanchy early in her headship was the relationship between the Christian and Jewish religions in the School. Tolerance of all races, creeds and religions had long been one of the School's outstanding strengths. The only concern in the late 1980s was that while the School recognised the Christian and Jewish faiths through the provision of separate assemblies, it had as yet done little to acknowledge the several faiths of the growing number of Asian girls. Mrs Clanchy undertook a review of the situation in the summer of 1986. It was felt that establishing further separate assemblies would not be in the best interests of the School as a whole but it was possible to strengthen the existing assemblies which 'should be a unifying force within a school'. While the right of parents to withdraw their child from any religious assembly would be maintained, as would the policy of the School in not asking the religion of prospective pupils, it was decided that there was no longer any reason why religious societies should not be formed. It was agreed to end the division between Christian and Jewish religious

An Indian evening in the mid-1990s.

education in the first three years of the Senior School, and to teach the subject to everyone together. For GCSE the subject became optional and a syllabus in Judaism was retained.

Another problem Joan Clanchy had to tackle soon after her appointment was the gentle decline in numbers at the School. These had fallen from 817 pupils in 1978 to 759 in 1986. More significantly, the School was losing some fifteen girls every year after they had taken their GCSEs as they left to take up sixth-form studies at boys' schools. Girls' schools were suffering from increasing competition with boys' schools as the latter sought to boost their numbers by taking in girls either at sixth-form level or even earlier. Fewer pupils also meant less revenue.

This situation was further complicated by the fact pointed out in 1987 that 'Despite the availability of bursaries, it had not been possible to maintain the same social mix as in the time of the Direct Grant . . . every effort should be made to publicise the availability of bursaries to those parents who had genuine need and perhaps had not even considered applying for the School on grounds of cost . . . insufficient entry applications came from local maintained schools.' The competition between schools was steadily driving up fees. Coupled with a declining interest from local primary schools in entering their pupils for the School, this inevitably affected the social composition of the School. For several years the School had fewer applicants for assisted places or bursaries than the number available.

Joan Clanchy wanted to combat falling numbers in several ways. Firstly, she wanted to move from a three-form entry at the age of 11 with thirty-one pupils in each class to a four-form entry with twenty-six in each class. This would expand the Senior School a little and also provide smaller classes. Secondly, she proposed moving an expanded Junior School into its own building, so that the younger girls could have more opportunities and form a strong cohort of well-prepared 11-year-olds for the Senior School, thus competing with rival schools. Thirdly, pastoral care needed to be improved in what was now called the Senior School. Fourthly, sixth-form life had to be made more attractive. And, fifthly, transportation problems had to be resolved.

The Junior School was completed in late 1987 and was officially opened by Princess Alice, the Duchess of Gloucester, on 18 February 1988. With its own hall and library, it brought all the junior forms together under their own roof for the first time. But taking girls from the age of 7 rather than 5 created difficulties for some parents. So in 1995 the opening of the First School for girls from 4 years upwards made it possible to offer parents complete continuity of education for their daughters.

If girls enjoyed their years up to taking their GCSEs, it was likely that they would choose to join the sixth form at the School rather than move elsewhere. Changing circumstances, linked to the growing pressures of

The burial of the time capsule at the opening of the First School in 1995.

examinations, made it essential that the system of pastoral care in the School was adapted to meet the needs of the pupils. This was an evolving process which, on the evidence of rising numbers, proved successful.

Going home, 1992.

Joan Clanchy's belief that life in the sixth form had to become more attractive to retain potential sixth-formers mirrored the conclusion that Kitty Anderson had reached after the Second World War. In fact, one of the measures taken was exactly the same and the attractive surroundings of the Old House were once more given over to the sixth form where private study rooms were also provided. Sixth-formers were given greater responsibility by placing them in charge of running the various societies. Sixth-form teaching was overhauled. And the first attempt was made to reform the prefect system. The main criticism of the system was the same as it had been forty years earlier. It created a small élite from whose privileges the great majority were precluded. Reform was supported by the staff but met strong opposition from the girls. It was only at the third attempt that prefects were abolished. All members of the upper sixth form then shared responsibilities in the School, led by a small senior students' committee.

Recruitment at the School was also hindered by the practical problem of home-to-school transport. There were instances of girls being bullied on the Underground, while Edgware station was more than a mile from the School. Growing traffic congestion made it more and more difficult for those parents some distance from the School to bring in their daughters. Other schools were already providing transport and for some parents this was now a deciding factor in their selection of a school. In 1987 the North London Collegiate School introduced with success its first coach for girls from the Hampstead area and within a year the School's coach scheme was well established. This initiative had a considerable beneficial effect on recruitment. It also strengthened community spirit, bringing together outside School girls from the same areas, often for the first time.

By the early 1990s, all these measures had seen an increase in the numbers of pupils. The Junior School was providing half of the annual intake for the Senior School. In the spring of 1992 there were 899 pupils at the School. This was in the depths of an economic recession and extensive use was now made of the bursary fund, as assistance was given to more and more girls already at the School to enable them to stay on. The roll in spring 1992 included almost one hundred girls with assisted places. But the recession obscured the fact that fewer bursaries were being awarded to new entrants to the School.

It was a time of growing competition between schools, a number of which were already adopting marketing techniques. Apart from academic results, the most tangible indication of progress within a school was the improvement and extension of the facilities it offered its pupils. At the North London Collegiate School, reserves had been exhausted by the construction

Two of the important improvements to the School in 1989: the new craft, design and technology centre (below), and the six all-weather tennis courts, opened by Sue Barker in 1989 (below right).

of the 'Octagon' and the Junior School so another appeal was launched to coincide with the 50th anniversary of the laying of the foundation stone for the new building at Canons in 1939. A sports hall was the main feature of the original list of developments intended to be funded by the appeal and a covered swimming pool was also considered but it was decided that other needs at the time were more pressing. These included a craft, design and technology centre (this subject was now part of the National Curriculum) which was to be converted from the former home economics room; an all-weather surface featuring six tennis courts combined with netball and lacrosse practice areas, which would go some way to improving the School's outdoor recreational facilities; and the modernisation of the science laboratories. All these aims were achieved and additional smaller projects were also able to go ahead thanks to the generosity of donors and trusts, including the Doris Gregory Trust.

The major project undertaken during Mrs Clanchy's time was the new swimming pool. The School had always had a shortage of indoor space for physical recreation and this was again pointed out on a visit to the School by an Old North Londoner, Eileen Alexander, the former principal of the Bedford College of Physical Education. She suggested that the best way to remedy this shortfall would be for a new indoor swimming pool to replace the outdated outdoor pool. Miss Alexander also very generously offered to donate substantially towards the costs of construction. A site was chosen close to the site of the old pool, work began in the summer of 1992 and was completed in the spring of 1993. Princess Alice visited the School once again to open the pool on 21 April 1993. It was hoped that at some future date the site adjacent to the swimming pool would be used for a sports hall which would be linked with the pool as one complex.

Mrs Clanchy also initiated the first phase of improvements to the School library which had been in need of modernisation for some time. Since the

The two major building projects of the 1990s: the new swimming pool (below left), and the McLauchlan Library, opened by Penelope Lively in 1999 (below).

McLauchlan Theatre was not well used, the Governors decided that the 'Octagon' should instead house a new library. Designed by an Old North Londoner, Pamela Lea (*née* Toyne), the first phase, occupying the top third of the building, was brought into use in 1991.

Looking to the future, Mrs Clanchy also recognised the need to raise additional funds for capital improvements. The new appeal, which was restricted to parents and friends of the School, had two main objectives. One was the erection of the proposed sports hall and the other was for the further restructuring and refurbishment of the library, including the installation of substantial information technology resources. The sports hall, boasting a huge multi-purpose hall and fitness centre, was completed during the summer of 1998 while the library, encapsulating the importance placed on the book as a medium for independent learning by both Mrs Clanchy and her successor, Mrs McCabe, of which more later, was opened by the author, Penelope Lively, in early 1999.

The School successfully sustained its outstanding academic record. This and much else in the School could not have been achieved without the commitment of the staff. One of Mrs Clanchy's innovations was a system of staff appraisal to provide a clearer sense of direction for the School. This was complemented by the introduction of a school development plan, setting out the aims and objectives of the School from year to year. In 1991 she also created a senior management team, including the recently appointed Bursar, Susan Meikle, to which she delegated responsibilities for running the school and which also acted as a valuable sounding board for a variety of issues.

But Mrs Clanchy recognised, as Miss McLauchlan had done, that greater emphasis on examination results was placing more pressure on girls to succeed. To combat this, there had been for several years no prizes (other

Annabel Croft unveils the plaque at the opening of the Canons Sports Centre in 1998 (below), and coaches some of the School's young players (below right).

Sports Day in the mid-1990s.

than leaving prizes) nor any orders of merit. Mrs Clanchy went further. Subject marks would no longer be compared with a norm, which made it possible for an entire class to be given A grades, and no scores would be given out. This was mocked in some quarters outside the School but the Head Mistress was adamant that the talents of all her students deserved to be recognised, something which her predecessors would have applauded.

The competitive pressure on girls increased as the Government placed more and more emphasis on results rather than education. This was a period of constant change in education, including the introduction of GCSEs and the National Curriculum, both of which the North London Collegiate School took in its stride. Then came the appearance, at first unofficially and then officially, of academic league tables in the early 1990s. The instinctive reaction of the Head Mistress was to oppose them but she discovered that many parents and Old North Londoners were expressing concern at the School's absence from the top of the tables. So the tables were used to shake the School out of any complacency there may have been and encourage a fresh approach towards learning in many departments. That did not prevent Mrs Clanchy from pointing out that 'the pressure on the students that the increasing attention given to results has created is largely destructive: nothing but an A is seen as respectable and many of our GCSE and A-level candidates are working too hard and worrying too much.' An excessive focus on results drove the Head Mistress to resign from membership of the National Curriculum Council over changes to the English curriculum in March 1993, writing to the Secretary of State for Education that 'the dominant aim has become a

A lesson in the School grounds.

curriculum designed for tests and the result is a model of English teaching which is barren and anti-intellectual.' In 1996 the Head Mistress could write that 'we are still at Canons trying to assert the right to a civilised life as well as GCSE.' Concern about examination successes was beginning to cloud the wider horizon which had been part of the School tradition for so long. In such circumstances the measures to relieve competitive pressure were both reasonable and sensible.

Many of the ingredients of life at the School continued as before with rising standards in drama and music, the birth of new societies, further expansion in sporting opportunities, sporting and cultural trips abroad, and the extension of exchange links with schools overseas. Music was thriving under a newly appointed director of music. Chamber music ensembles were achieving outstanding competitive success in the National Chamber Music Competition while the School orchestra was flourishing and there was a wealth of vocal talent. Senior societies were given a fixed slot on Thursday afternoons without the distraction of any other activities to ensure that visiting speakers were heard by as many girls as possible. While the relationship with the Goethe Gymnasium in Ludwigsburg remained as strong as ever, new links were forged by the sixth form with the Institution Join Lambert in Rouen and by members of staff with the Germantown Academy in Philadelphia. Emily Wagner from the Academy discovered from the time she spent at the School that 'diversity is respected and encouraged. There is a seriousness of purpose tempered by a strong respect and sense of co-operation between teachers and students. The entire school community really seems to enjoy the learning process and being with one another.' An interesting exchange for a BBC television programme took place between two pupils from the School and Rook Heath Comprehensive School. The pupil from Rook Heath, Tara McBride, felt that the schools were not as different as she had expected although

Just three of the many musical activities at the school. Above: *the junior orchestra;* below: *the 1998 Canons Follies, which have become a tradition since the first production in 1976;* below right: *a Senior piano trio; North London Collegiate were national prizewinners for seven consecutive years.*

'the attitude of the pupils were undoubtedly different. In particular, I found that the pupils at NLCS were definitely more determined to succeed . . . more readily prepared to study.' Charlotte Edgeworth from the School agreed, having found at Rook Heath that 'there was less discipline so pupils did not pay as much attention.' Both girls enjoyed themselves although Charlotte felt that in the end the programme 'does little to abolish or even change stereotypes but instead enforces them.'

The School also took seriously its traditional responsibility for promoting greater opportunities for young women. At a colloquium at the School arranged in 1990, one of the guest speakers, Mary Archer, pointed out that 'women will really have arrived when there are as many mediocre and average women at the top as there are now mediocre and average men.' Baroness Warnock, Mistress of Girton, emphasised that equality of success was now as important as equality of opportunity: 'It is not enough, if justice is to be done, to ensure that everyone has a chance to enter the competition for the glittering prizes, if, as the competition proceeds, it becomes clear that some of the competitors are being actively prevented from winning.' She felt that in the 1990s as in the 1850s an apparent concern for women and their femininity was being used both by men and women to deny success to many women. But Old North Londoners were still making their mark in areas once the preserve of men. In 1991 Helen Stone became only the third woman to become a Fellow of the Institute of Civil Engineers while in the following year Chella Franklin became the first woman to be appointed to serve on a ship in the Royal Navy when she joined HMS *Norfolk*. In the spring of 1994 Barbara Baisley (*née* More) was one of the first women to be ordained in the Church of England.

When Joan Clanchy decided to retire in 1997, she wrote for the purposes of her speech at her final assembly an open letter for posterity to her eight-month-old grandson in which she said that 'I have worked for twelve years in a really lovely school' with its 'tradition of having outgoing, talkative, bouncy girls'. The Chairman of Governors at the time, Norma Rinsler (*née* Lee), an Old North Londoner, wrote that Mrs Clanchy had helped to preserve the traditions of the School while moving it forward. In this she had much in common with her predecessors, each of whom had upheld the tradition which Isabella Drummond had described as 'constant change and development' combined with 'a continuity of personality' where continuity was achieved by 'the overlapping of generations'. Joan Clanchy had achieved much in her twelve years at the School. As Norma Rinsler remarked, 'When she has a clear idea of what she wants to achieve, she does not accept constraints without a fight.' On the other hand, the warmth of her personality combined with her acute sensitivity to the needs of others had enlarged the ethos of the School. As she said in her address on Founder's Day in 1988, 'If education is to mean more than a collection of certificates, service must still be our ideal.'

A photography weekend workshop, 1999.

Medusa – *a costume produced for the fantasy fashion show in 1998.*

133

Bernice McCabe, Head Mistress since 1997.

Sixth-formers at work in the Buss Library (which was set aside for their sole use at Mrs McCabe's initiative), under the watchful gaze of the School's founder.

Her successor, Bernice McCabe, came to the School from the headship of Chelmsford County High School for Girls, a grant-maintained school, where she had earned the reputation for turning it into the leading state school in the country. She had been educated at Clifton High School in Bristol which had been founded in 1877 along the lines pioneered by Frances Mary Buss and developed by the Girls' Public Day School Trust. After reading English at university, she had spent twenty-three years teaching in the state sector. In 1986 she joined The Heathland School, Hounslow, as deputy head where she was inspired by the whole ethos of the school. Here was a school whose pupils were below average ability yet their self-esteem and examination results were excellent. Staff and pupils were encouraged to have the highest expectations. Academic excellence was not promoted at the expense of excellence in other spheres where achievement was also applauded. Staff were also encouraged to participate in the running of the school – a large number of them subsequently went on to obtain headships elsewhere.

Bernice McCabe was one of them. When she joined Chelmsford County High School for Girls in 1990, it was a school with a great tradition with committed staff and lively girls but without the results to match its potential. Mrs McCabe took time to listen to pupils, parents and staff, discerning the values which were part of the school's character, and arriving at aims and priorities for the future. Building on the lessons she had learnt at The Heathland School, she created a team around her through whom she implemented the school's priorities and to whom she delegated responsibilities. Like Mrs Clanchy, she used the appearance of league tables to stimulate a revival of academic commitment. The circumstances of the school demanded that competition should be emphasised. All this paid off. In 1994 the school was among the first to be inspected by the Office for Standards in Education (Ofsted). It was described as an outstandingly successful school and particular mention was made of the systematic approach to the development of the school by the head. In seven years Mrs McCabe and her staff turned Chelmsford County High School for Girls from the lowest placed Essex grammar school in the league tables to the most successful of all state schools.

Young, self-assured and poised, Bernice McCabe was energetic and perceptive, idealistic and decisive. Being a good listener helped to give her a clear sense of direction and the art of delegation came easily to her. She regarded the involvement of staff and pupils in the running of schools as a positive benefit which ought to be encouraged.

The challenge she faced when she arrived as Head Mistress of the North London Collegiate School in 1997 was rather different from that which had confronted her at Chelmsford. Here was a school with many strengths which was already well established among the leading academic schools in the country. As she had at Chelmsford, Mrs McCabe took time to listen to pupils, parents, staff and governors. She found the girls were motivated but perfectionist. The examiners' reports she sought out provided evidence that students preferred to take a cautious approach to their work, being more willing to regurgitate the knowledge they had absorbed in class than to take risks and employ it independently. Mrs McCabe concluded that the challenge was to encourage the girls to fulfil their potential by thinking more for themselves. She wanted to build on the tradition common both to the North London Collegiate and to Clifton High School which instilled in girls the belief that there was nothing which they could not achieve. Her guiding principle, she wrote, had always been 'the importance of having high expectations and of never "writing anyone off".' She wanted to ensure that the potential of each girl was never under-valued, that even those in difficulties were given the encouragement to exceed previous expectations.

But she also believed that academic achievements had to be balanced against the development of self-confidence, of self-esteem and of a sense of enjoyment in everything that her students undertook. 'It is important to me,' Mrs McCabe wrote, 'that every girl develops the self-confidence to believe that she can make a difference to the world when she leaves NLCS.'

She felt that 'Once a girl comes to this school we have to show her what she is good at. Everybody has talents. The function of this school is to give them a chance to fly.' For Mrs McCabe the development of academic confidence in the girls meant moving them away from the belief that the purpose of all study was examination results and showing them that it was not only possible but pleasurable to develop a love of knowledge for its own sake. The practical side of this philosophy was reflected in the new library. Mrs McCabe, working with the architect, Pamela Lea, was closely involved in the design of the extended library with other members of her staff, with the girls and with every section of the School community. Typically, the committee formed for this purpose was chaired not by the Head Mistress but by a senior member of staff. It was agreed that the library should mirror the aims of the School to encourage a love of learning and scholarship. The girls agreed that the new library, unlike its predecessor, should be a place of quiet and calm. The library was extended to fill the whole of the 'Octagon'. It provided comfortable chairs in a light and airy environment, with attractive views from the library's windows down the lime avenue. The original utilitarian treatment of the spiral staircase was replaced by a more striking combination of stainless steel and glass and the library boasted a mezzanine floor, 600 metres of shelving, and the latest information technology. At Mrs McCabe's initiative, the Buss Library then became a specialist library for the sixth form.

In addition, the School would continue to provide extensive opportunities for the girls to develop their self-confidence in other areas. The Head Mistress believed that it was essential to continue to extend the breadth of

A sixth-form chemistry experiment.

The computer network offers access to the school intranet as well as the internet.

135

extra-curricular activities available to girls at the School. There is no doubt that they have every chance of achieving this at the North London Collegiate School. The list in recent years has included drama, music, visits to art galleries in London and Paris, a wide range of sporting activities, the Duke of Edinburgh award scheme, the Young Enterprise scheme, field trips in the UK and a variety of visits overseas, regular debates, distinguished guest speakers, conferences, competitions and community service. The Head Mistress was eager to see drama given as much emphasis as music within the School. Upon the opening of the sports hall, the former west gymnasium was converted into a studio theatre, known as 'The Black Box', which is regarded as another step on the way to the creation of a proper school theatre. An additional drama specialist was appointed to the staff and the number of drama productions has already multiplied. Another significant move by the new Head Mistress which emphasised her belief in developing the potential talent of her students was the appointment of a new head of art who combined the School tradition of concentrating on technique with an emphasis on liberating the latent gifts of his pupils.

Mrs McCabe also believed as strongly as her predecessors that it must remain possible for able girls from disadvantaged backgrounds to attend the School whose distinctive character has always been shaped by including girls from different cultural and social backgrounds. The abolition of the Assisted Places Scheme from the autumn of 1998 placed this at risk since the School has never been in a sufficiently strong financial position to rely solely upon its own bursaries and scholarships to perpetuate this integral part of its ethos. To place the provision of such financial assistance on a more sure footing, the Governors launched a £2 million bursary fund appeal to coincide with the celebration of the School's 150th anniversary.

She also wanted to ensure that her gifted and dedicated staff enjoyed opportunities to develop their own careers both inside the School and beyond it. For example, vacancies for internal posts were thrown open to all applicants, an induction course was established for new staff and a series of voluntary professional development posts were offered on a short-term basis for staff who wished to broaden their experience. At the same time she expanded the system of continuous staff appraisal. The development plan became a more sophisticated and systematic process, involving the whole School and deeply rooted in every significant area of the institution. All parents receive a summary of the plan and are invited to attend an annual presentation on the evaluation of its implementation.

By any standards, including those set by the School itself throughout its history, the North London Collegiate School is an outstanding institution which continues to build on its inheritance. It was particularly appropriate that as the School approached its 150th anniversary in the summer of 1999 it achieved the best academic results in the country, 94.2 per cent of the

One of the School's many drama productions in recent years: Cabaret, produced in 1999.

School's A level students achieving A and B grades, and was named by a national newspaper as Independent School of the Year.

The widespread interest its reputation attracts today continues to reflect the School's notable place in education established when Frances Mary Buss first opened the doors of her new institution. Her death in 1894 received national coverage with extensive obituaries in newspapers national, regional and local, such had been her accepted impact on English education. In 1938 news of Nazi activity in Poland played a supporting role in some newspapers to the report and accompanying illustration of the move of the School to Canons. One of its most illustrious former pupils, Marie Stopes, who recently gained the accolade of being one of the Women of the Millennium, often paid tribute to the benign influence of her School.

Affection for the School and the continuation of lasting friendships characterise the Old North Londoners' Association, a thriving organisation which provides substantial support to the School. The ONLA is one part of a strong community which as well as Governors, teaching and non-teaching staff and pupils also includes parents whose own organisation, the Parents' Guild, undertakes many fund-raising activities for the School and organises a wide range of social events.

The examination results in the summer of 1999 maintained a tradition of excellence. Perhaps one of the secrets of this success lies in the way in which the principles laid down by that astonishing woman, Frances Mary Buss, have remained intact while being adapted to the needs of different generations. She herself believed in constant improvement, a theme to which each of her successors has been committed. Miss Drummond summed it up as a 'constant change and development' without weakening the traditions of the School.

What are these traditions? The first is an expectation of the highest

Above left: sketching in the Rodin Museum gardens during an art trip to Paris in 1992; above: Sir David Attenborough at the unveiling of the Wildlife Mural in 1994.

Making a stained-glass window – a yearly project each Christmas.

Tobogganing in the early 1990s.

standards from every girl. Allied to this has been a consistent encouragement of a spirit of self-reliance and enterprise among the girls, that they should think things out for themselves. Miss Drummond, who worked hard to dispel the notion that some subjects were beyond the capabilities of the average girl, was not alone in discovering that the result was a steady improvement in standards of work. Such standards have been founded upon a teaching staff of outstanding calibre. Miss Buss was as responsible as anyone for creating a profession out of teaching. Not only did she insist on qualifications and training for teachers, she fostered their personal development while on the staff of the School, encouraging them to move on to better things when the chance arose. Her successors have followed her example and over the years have also displayed a gift for appointing individuals whose talent for teaching has gained praise from inspectors and pupils alike.

The School has sought as far as possible to draw out the potential of every girl, 'to help a girl to find her own special gifts', as Miss Drummond put it. The circumstances of the School's foundation and the time it took before the same opportunities in higher education were available to young women as well as to young men meant that the School was sometimes accused of an overemphasis upon the achievements of the academically most able. But this should not detract from the fact that at every stage of its history, the aim of the School has been to prepare young women for their full potential in whatever sphere of activity they pursued in the wider world.

Another important part of the School's ethos is a determination not to cramp a girl's education to meet the requirements of examinations. Examinations are undoubtedly important and one of Miss Buss's great achievements was in enabling girls to have their educational performance measured according to the same standards as boys. But much more important has been the School's desire to encompass what Sophie Bryant called 'the worldwide horizon of the child's natural desire for knowledge'. At one time or another Sophie Bryant, Isabella Drummond, Kitty Anderson, Madeline McLauchlan, Joan Clanchy and Bernice McCabe have all recognised, to paraphrase Dame Kitty, that the purpose of education should not be sacrificed for the sake of competition.

At the North London Collegiate School the importance of examinations has been put into perspective by expanding the opportunities available to girls both inside and outside the classroom. Miss Buss began the ethic of social service which continues to find practical expression at the School. Miss Drummond enlarged the freedom of the girls by removing restrictive rules and giving them the chance to take up new responsibilities through the prefects or through running the many societies. These societies in their range and quality have played an important part in opening a window on the world for North Londoners at a school which has always had a reputation for looking outwards. Through the introduction of general studies, Miss Harold introduced many girls for the first time to the sheer delight of intellectual study. Dame Kitty widened social opportunities through joint ventures with neighbouring boys' schools. During Miss McLauchlan's time, the liberating advantages of foreign travel became widely available. Mrs Clanchy and Mrs McCabe have both overseen the enhancement of intellectual and physical opportunities. Yet the names in this paragraph are almost interchangeable, for the principles which have guided any one of these Head Mistresses have been the principles which have guided them all.

Another important strand of the North London tradition is the desire, no matter how difficult the circumstances, that the education provided by the School should be available to those able to take advantage of it, regardless of their personal circumstances. So the School under Miss Buss strove to maintain modest fees and to offer scholarships despite the lack of any endowments; and under Mrs McCabe it has launched the biggest appeal in its history directed specifically at providing financial assistance for future talented pupils from less affluent backgrounds. In the same vein, the School has always had a consistent reputation for practising social, religious and racial tolerance.

When Joan Clanchy remarked that 'if education is to mean more than a collection of certificates, service must still be our ideal', her words encapsulated the work of the School over nearly a century and a half, reflecting the balance always to be struck between education focused on examinations and the qualifications they bring and education as a preparation of the whole person for future life. The success of the North London Collegiate School continues to be in striking that balance while providing an educational environment characterised by the warmth, liveliness, vitality and zest of the girls themselves.

It was as long ago as 1887 that one school inspector told Miss Buss that he had known for some years that the North London Collegiate School was 'the best girls' school in England'. That accolade could be applied with little sense of exaggeration throughout the School's entire history.

Three friends by the pond.

Sources and Bibliography

The list below is not exhaustive but gives the sources which have been most useful for the preparation of this history.

North London Collegiate School Magazine, 1875–
ONLine, 1995–, Old North Londoners' magazine
Governors' Minutes, 1875–
Prize Day Reports, 1850–1939
School Prospectuses, 1850–

Reminiscences: Chapter 2 – Lottie Armstead; Chapter 3 – Pamela Riggs (*née* Hailey), Peggy Cohda (*née* Martin), Margaret Guy, Margaret Carpenter, Maureen van Horn, Ethel Howie, Doris McCarthy, Maria Kosloff, Ann Miller; Chapter 4 – Pamela Riggs (*née* Hailey), Pat Shirley (*née* O'Sullivan), Charlotte Franklin (*née* Hajnal-Konji), Barbara Dorf, Janet Mellors; Chapter 5 – *The Class of 1971 – Twenty Years On*

Board of Education, Reports of Inspections, 1903, 1910, 1914, 1926, 1937 and 1958
London County Council, Report of Full Inspection, 1921
'The Education of Girls': an address delivered at the annual conference of the National Association of Inspectors of Schools & Educational Organisations on 5 October 1951 by Dr K Anderson
'Frances Mary Buss: her role in the education of women': an address delivered as part of the sesquicentenary of the North London Collegiate School on 12 October 1999 by Marilyn Strathern, Mistress of Girton College, Cambridge
School archive files on Miss Buss, Mrs Bryant, Miss Drummond, Miss Harold, Dame Kitty Anderson, Miss McLauchlan, Mrs Clanchy and Mrs McCabe

Allen, Edith, *Unpublished Memoirs*
Archer, R. L., *Secondary Education in the Nineteenth Century*, London, 1966
Avery, G., *The Best Type of Girl: a history of girls' independent schools*, London, 1991
Bryant, Sophie, DSc., Litt.D., 1850–1922, *North London Collegiate School*, London, 1922
Burstall, S., *Education of Girls & Women in Great Britain*, London, 1897
Burstall, S., *Frances Mary Buss, an Educational Pioneer*, London, 1938
Burstall, S., *Retrospect and Prospect: Sixty Years of Women's Education*, London, 1933
Crow, D., *The Victorian Woman*, London, 1971
Digby, A., & Searle, P., *Children, School and Society in Nineteenth Century England*, London, 1981
Hobbs, P., ed., *Memories of North London Collegiate School in Wartime (1939–45)*, Edgware, 1995
Hughes, M. V., *A London Girl of the Eighties*, London, 1936
Kamm, J., *How Different From Us*, London, 1958
Mumford, Edith E. Read, *Through Rose-Coloured Spectacles*, Leicester, 1952
Price, M., & Glenday, N., *Reluctant Revolutionaries: A Century of Headmistresses 1874–1974*, London, 1974
Ridley, A., *Frances Mary Buss and Her Work in Education*, London, second edition, 1896
Schools Inquiry Commission, 1, Parliamentary Papers (1867–8) XXVIII, part 1
Toplis, G., ed., *Leaves from the Note-Books of Frances Mary Buss*, London, 1896

Index

Page numbers in *italics* refer to illustrations. ***Bold italic*** numbers refer to colour plates on an unpaginated facing page.

Picture Acknowledgements

Camden Local Studies and Archives Centre 60 (bottom); The Cheltenham Ladies' College 20 (bottom); Girton College, Cambridge 27; Hulton Getty 93; Imperial War Museum 62; London Borough of Barnet Archives 88 (top); Mary Evans Picture Library 12 (top), 47 (bottom); National Portrait Gallery 12 (bottom), 13 (top), 79 (top), 100; Tim Rawle Associates 2, facing page 73, facing page 96, facing page 120, 129 (left), 132 (top), 134, 135, 136; Roger Tabraham 125 (bottom), 126, 127, 128 (left), 131 (top), 132 (bottom left), 133, 137 (top left), 138, 139 (top). All other pictures are taken from the North London Collegiate School archives.

New photography of NLCS archive material and paintings by David Lambert Photography.

New photography of the School grounds by John Spragg.

ISBN 0 907 383 300

First published in 2000
© North London Collegiate School 2000

Project Editor and Designer: Susannah McSkimming
Printed and bound by Butler & Tanner, Frome, Somerset

Published by
James & James (Publishers) Ltd
Gordon House Business Centre
6 Lissenden Gardens
London NW5 1LX